WASA
GOS

WASABI GOSPEL

the startling message of Jesus
SHAWN WOOD

Abingdon Press
Nashville

WASABI GOSPEL
THE STARTLING MESSAGE OF JESUS

Copyright © 2009 by Abingdon Press

This book is printed on acid-free paper.

Library of Congress Cataloging-in-Publication Data

Wood, Shawn.
Wasabi gospel : the startling message of Jesus / Shawn Wood.
    p.   cm.
ISBN 978-1-4267-0050-7 (pbk. : alk. paper)
1. Christian life—Biblical teaching.   2. Jesus Christ—Teachings.   I. Title.

BS2417.C5W66   2009
248.4—dc22

2009009568

09 10 11 12 13 14 15 16 17 18—10 9 8 7 6 5 4 3 2

MANUFACTURED IN THE UNITED STATES OF AMERICA

To Connie, There has never been a man who loved a woman more than I love you. This and everything I do is dedicated to you.

To Isabelle. You have your daddy where you want him. You are my princess, and I have been irreversibly changed by your smile.

To Hayes. I needed a boy in the house to balance the power. You are my new little buddy, and I look forward to many stories about you in future books.

CONTENTS

ACKNOWLEDGMENTS ix

INTRODUCTION xi

LAURA'S STORY: PART ONE 1

CHAPTER ONE 5
God, I'll Take the Mercy, but Give the Idiot Who Cut Me Off in Traffic Justice

LAURA'S STORY: PART TWO 21

CHAPTER TWO 25
Are You Sure You're Allowed to Do That?

LAURA'S STORY: PART THREE 41

CHAPTER THREE 45
I Have to Love Osama Too?

LAURA'S STORY: PART FOUR 61

CHAPTER FOUR 65
Rich People Go Straight to Hell, Do Not Pass Go

LAURA'S STORY: PART FIVE   81

CHAPTER FIVE   85
Jesus, Were You the First Mobster?

LAURA'S STORY: PART SIX   99

CHAPTER SIX   103
What If I Use a Rearview Mirror?

LAURA'S STORY: PART SEVEN   119

CHAPTER SEVEN   123
**So—Jesus, What Happens When I
Don't Have Any Limbs Left to Cut Off?**

CONCLUSION   141

ACKNOWLEDGMENTS

I am thirty-five years old. If there is one thing I know, it is that I am not the wisest individual on earth, and it would be ridiculous for me to write or live as though I were.

I have gained so much information from listening to sermons of my favorite preachers that it is often hard to even give credit as I have tried to glean so much from them. To list is difficult, but list I must as there are just a few that have made an incredible impact on me.

Greg Surratt is not only my pastor, my friend, and my mentor but he is also an amazing communicator. His name should be on the cover of this book alongside mine, as I have learned so much from him over the last eight years of listening to him preach at Seacoast and watching him live before me.

Each week while I run on the treadmill I listen to Matt Chandler and Mark Driscoll. They are my podcast pastors, and I am becoming more like the Jesus they preach because of them.

My author friends. Gary Ezzo and Geoff Surratt have been available to answer all of my really naive and important questions about being an author. It is good to have friends.

Ashley Hair is the best designer in the world. Bar none. She will design every book I write, and she makes Seacoast pretty too.

Katie Hann, your insight, writing, and help on Laura's story gave life and feeling to them that I could never have given without you.

My fellow Experiences teammates at Seacoast: Ashley, Katie, Megan, Sarah, and Steve.

The Abingdon team, especially my editor, Jessica Kelley. Jessica and I write together using Google Docs. She gets me. She anticipates when I am in a slump. She knows when I need an e-mail of encouragement, and most of all she helps me get the message of Jesus into words in a better way.

And last to Craig Groeschel and Andy Stanley on the subject of money. I can be very clear where much of my influence for chapter 4 has come from. In 2006 Andy Stanley did a series at North Point Community Church; I listened to every word, several times. In 2007 Craig Groeschel at Lifechurch.tv gave Andy credit for a great series and presented similar material; I listened to every word, several times. In 2008 Greg Surratt took this same material, and I helped make it a Seacoast message series and listened to every word, several times. To try to write about money without giving these three men credit would be impossible for me.

I love Asian food.

One of the reasons that I run sixteen miles a week and lift heavy things at the gym is my love for General Tso's chicken.

I also love hanging out with people. I am an introvert who likes to be exhausted. (If you understand what I mean, you are probably one too.)

Finally, I love new and eclectic foods. I will try just about anything once.

Put all of these together on a Thursday night in 1996, and you have the makings of a great story. And don't we all love a great story?

I had just taken a position at a church as their Singles and Recreation Pastor. Having been single all of about fifteen minutes in my life clearly made me the ideal candidate. In fact at the ripe old age of twenty-two, I was celebrating my second anniversary of being happily married to the only girl I ever dated for more than a month.

As you can see, I was made to be a *singles* pastor.

Being new to the church, I really wanted to meet some people and I found out that there was a group of singles who went out for Japanese food once a month, and they invited the new pastor to come along. This proved to be an interesting evening.

As we were browsing the menu, the waitress came around and asked if anyone would like something from the sushi menu. Now you need to understand that I am from the Low Country of South Carolina. We eat a lot of fish and a lot of shrimp. We can catch the stuff in our own backyards. I even ate crawdads out of a ditch more than once as a child, which may explain a lot. But all of the aforementioned crustaceans and swimming beasts were cooked (including the crawdads)!

Sushi had just made its way to the South, another invasion of Northern Aggression, and everyone around me was pressuring me to try some—as if I were a teenager getting ready to drink his first beer. But as I said, I will try anything once, so I ordered me up some dead, raw fish. Not so appealing if you call it like it is, is it?

I have always wondered if the Japanese, with their penchant for great electronics, have hidden cameras in these restaurants to capture silly Americans eating dead, raw fish for the first time. If so, they should start a show. It would be a ratings giant. Especially if this night had been caught on camera.

They brought out my plate of what appeared to be some shrimp that had lost a battle with a blob of rice, and set it in front of me. Everyone was talking and laughing and enjoying their sushi, so I was on my own to take my time. Off to the side of the plate, there was a small little dollop of what appeared to be Japanese butter. Cute.

For some reason they had dyed it green, who knows why, but that was not my primary concern.

If it had been 2009 rather than 1996, I would have figured it was one of the more wild-haired offshoots of the "green" movement, but since it was 1996 I figured the Japanese just liked their butter a little on the molded side. I had eaten blue cheese, so why not green butter?

When you are getting ready to eat dead, raw fish—who cares about the color of the butter? However, one thing I have learned in the South is that butter can cover a multitude of sins and tasteless food. So like any red-blooded American, I spread every bit of that green Japanese butter on top of my shrimp, got it real close to my mouth, inhaled, and shoved it in.

There are not sufficient words in the English language to describe the amount of shock that enveloped my body. It was as if liquid lava were being created in my throat and mouth and all oxygen had been taken out of the air while Ultimate Fighting Champion Randy Couture beat me in the throat and gut. As I sat gasping for air I felt as though I might never be the same again. It was as if I were in the middle of a bad dream where everyone around me is moving in slow motion and I cannot communicate with them. I tried to let people know that I might have just eaten lava, but I could not breathe much less talk. Involuntary tears began to run down my cheeks, and life as I knew it stopped for just a few moments. Cute little Japanese butter. Also known as *wasabi*.

If you have eaten wasabi, you are commiserating with me and laughing as well. It's all good—laugh away. I lived.

If you have not eaten wasabi, just imagine blending habanero and jalapeño peppers in your Cuisinart, mixing that into a jar of horseradish, then adding some actual liquid fire for good measure, and you will get the picture.

This small, innocent, seemingly insignificant, cute little dollop was actually a concentrated, power-packed, punch-you-in-the-gut, life-altering experience.

I have never forgotten that moment.

Close to ten years later, while I was reading some of the words of Jesus, I had a similar experience. I was studying the Bible, just minding my own business, when a small, innocent, seemingly insignificant, cute little dollop of scripture I had read many, many times before became a concentrated, power-packed, punch-you-in-the-gut, life-altering experience. I had read the words many times before. They were cute. They were innocent and seemingly insignificant. Then it hit me. It almost startled me what Jesus was saying. I took a shot to the spiritual gut that rocked my world and made me realize that this tiny bit of scripture was actually a wasabi-punch to my soul. It changed my life. It was as if Jesus' words had just slapped me in the face, and I wondered—should I turn the other cheek?

I have never forgotten that moment.

On a quest to really examine the words of Jesus and their impact on our lives, this book will look at several small scriptures that pack a very big punch.

I pray it takes your breath away.

April 23

The rumor is that he adored me when I was really young--I've even seen evidence to that in pictures of us laughing and kissing. Someone who didn't know any better might look at those pictures and assume we were the type of father and daughter who would grow up to be friends, meeting regularly for coffee, reminiscing over the good times, smiling over the latest antics of the grandkids. But like I said, that's only if they didn't know any better. I don't remember ever feeling loved by him, and we've certainly never met for coffee.

It all started when I was about thirteen years old. Now, _abuse_ is a strong word, and I'm not really big on calling it that. I usually prefer to say something more along the lines of, "My dad and I had creative differences." Seems pretty benign when you put it that way versus the <u>abuse</u> word, doesn't it? A little more normal, a little less Lifetime Original Movie.

I'm going to be honest: I know that I definitely wasn't the perfect child, and I wasn't even a decent teenager. I'm old enough now to know that I brought on a whole lot of the trouble in my life. I don't know what did it, but I woke up one day and something had changed. I was a teenager not with just a rebellious streak––I was a teenager with a death wish. From that point on my father and I fought over everything. And I mean <u>everything.</u>

You know, the thing that still gets me is that I was only thirteen! And though I was a crazy, wild, troubled thirteen, I was still a kid nonetheless. Shouldn't it have been the parents' job to be the mature ones? What kind of father would . . . well, OK, so I still have a lot of rather strong feelings about it, if you can't tell.

I hate to say it, because I like to think of myself as independent and unique, but from that point on I became a cliché: a teenage girl with daddy issues running into the arms of bad boys who will pay attention to her. Yep, I was that girl. But at the time, it didn't seem like a cliché. In my thirteen-year-old mind, if I could just get the right boy to love me, everything would work out all right.

Looking back on it from my thirty-three-year-old standpoint, I can see that I was using the boys just as much as they were using me. Suppose it was a win-win situation--I would give them what they wanted, and it got me what I wanted: attention, something passing for love, and a way to infuriate my dad.

I can still remember lying in my bed at night, my stomach in knots, listening to my mom and dad yelling at each other, mostly about me. I still remember taking off out the back door and running as fast as I could after yet another screaming match with my dad, trying to get somewhere, anywhere else. And I still remember the first time that he called me a whore.

There are only so many times you can hear something about yourself before you begin forgetting if it's even true or not. Before it starts leaving some scars. Even by the end of eighth grade, I felt like I could trace those scars all over my body, like I had been cut to pieces and put back together again all wrong:

Scars from the pain of feeling unloved.

Scars from the pleasure that I sought and found empty.

Scars from the possibility that life would be this way forever.

So today, when I went off at the lady at Walmart because she had some trouble processing my return (turns out I bought it at Target--yep, I felt like a jerk), it wasn't really about her. And yesterday, when my friend Cindy called and said she forgot about our lunch date, the anger and resentment weren't really about her. The feelings just seem to come out of nowhere. But I know they're not coming from nowhere--they come from all the bitterness that's built up over the years. All of this is just the scar tissue from the pain that my dad caused me. He's ruined my life, and I don't know how I can ever forgive him.

My friend has talked me into going to this church (I guess she noticed I need some help with the bitterness too). The pastor said that God can heal us of our past. But how? How do I rid myself of this bitterness and anger that have tainted every aspect of my life? I've become a cliché--one of those sad stereotypes of brokenness and bitterness. I don't want to be a cliché! I <u>want</u> to forgive. I just don't know how.

CHAPTER ONE

God, I'll Take the Mercy, but Give the Idiot Who Cut Me Off in Traffic Justice

Blessed are the merciful,
for they will be shown mercy.
Matthew 5:7

I was minding my own business. I really was.

I had been assigned to teach on a pretty familiar scripture in our study of the Sermon on the Mount. It was a passage that I had read a million times.

It was then that I had a wasabi moment. A scripture that seemed so disarmingly cute and benign exploded in my spiritual stomach. It was as if Jesus' words slapped me in the face. I know for some of you that may seem a little harsh, but when you are as stubborn as I am you need to get slapped in the face every now and then.

Here is the verse that rocked me:

Blessed are the merciful, for they will be shown mercy.
Matthew 5:7

It's a little verse—ten words long, simple enough for even a fifth grader to understand. And although it's hard for those who know me best to believe, I am smarter than a fifth grader. I understood this verse, but as Mark Twain said, "It ain't those parts of the Bible that I can't understand that bother me, it is the parts that I do understand."

This mercy statement is one of those. It sounds so nice. I think I had always believed that all that Jesus was saying was, "Be nice and help people and, if you do, you will be helped too" (Shawn Revised Version).

Now that's an easy statement. That's a butter statement—easy to swallow, tastes good going down, and makes you fat and happy.

I like butter statements. I like the teachings of Jesus being churned down to an easy-to-swallow action step that I can add to the top of my already fat life as a spiritual topping. I guess sometimes I just don't like getting slapped with the truth of what Jesus is really saying.

But what I read was not butter. It was wasabi. Here is what I think that Jesus is really saying: "When someone hurts you in the worst kind of way, and when they owe you more than they could ever pay back, and even when they show no hint of being at all sorry—let them off the hook. You know why? Because that is what I did for you" (Shawn's Better Revised Version).

Do What?

Do you ever have that reaction when you read scripture? "Do what?"

As soon as my oldest child, Isabelle, was able to talk, she became the "Do what?" queen. Anytime she walked into a room and saw anything at all different than she expected (and she has her mom's OCD, so this happens pretty often) she would say in her perfect little Southern drawl, "Doooo whaaaat?" That's the reaction I had as Jesus' slap to the face and subsequent punch to the gut began to sink in. This is not the Jesus I had in mind.

I often find that when I read scripture I expect to see words that support ideas and beliefs I already hold. Wouldn't it be nice if everything in scripture were to line up just like we need it to? Like God wrote the Bible to confirm to us that we are indeed as righteous as think we are? If you are like me, you want to get a pat on the back when you forgive the forgivable. But I reserve the right to be able to hate people that hate me, love people that love me, take revenge on, those that I want revenge on, and hold a grudge against anyone who hurts me or anyone I know (or at least anyone I like—hurt my enemies all you want). That may sound selfish to you (and it is), but many times it's the truth for me, and I'm betting for some of you too.

Then I realized that I had to teach about this text the following weekend. That is a difficult place to be. I have a long-standing rule against lying when I preach. So, in an attempt not to get myself struck by lightning, I read over and over the statement above and asked myself the hardest question that someone can ask themselves when studying the Bible: "How can I live this out?" It was a time of letting the Bible read me a little rather than me just reading the Bible. Those are usually some very cool times.

Suddenly, God placed a name in my mind. It was the name of someone who had hurt me and many people whom I love very much in the worst kind of way. This person took advantage of a member of my family. This person destroyed people's lives and as I watched this person feel seemingly no remorse nor make any amends, I had to be honest. Not only did I not want to give this person mercy and forgiveness, I wanted to hurt this person back.

Have you ever been there? Many of you are probably there right now in your life. You are a Christ-follower and in 99 percent of your life you are striving to serve Jesus. You are taking next steps to get closer to him; you are growing your marriage; you are becoming a great parent; you are striving to be a great friend. All is well.

But there is that one area.

You know the area.

The area that you just let sit in the corner of your soul and it's dark, and it's neglected—that's the area that God is concerned with. It's also often the hardest part of our life for us to handle.

Right now some of you are experiencing some of the Holy Spirit poking and prodding that I was experiencing. With that last prod now I am thinking to myself that I really meant that whole "how can I apply this to my life?" thing as a rhetorical question to God. You cannot possibly mean that *he* deserves my mercy? I started making a list in my mind of all of the people I had forgiven, of all of the good will I had shown to others, of all of the areas of my life that were good to go to try and tip the scales of my justice and allow me to continue to hate this individual a little longer.

I have to admit that I have not learned much from forgiveness and mercy by actually living it out on my own. I am not very good at it. I think I inherited the ability to hold a grudge genetically or something. I am a true Southerner; we hold grudges pretty well.

But there have been people in my life who have gone before me who I have seen turn the other cheek, even when they could have won the battle. I have tried my best to learn from them and watch the way that they have responded to their enemies.

I remember watching as my grandfather consistently spoke highly of a man who had mistreated him and lied to him about the promises of a business deal, only to go another direction after my grandfather had turned down other offers. This was a life-changing lie that I witnessed when I was a young boy. But my grandfather never spoke a bad word about his offenders. In fact, I only saw him heap praises on them. I also watched him die never having received restitution or payment for that wrong. You know what I learned? It was not on his mind and never affected his life because he had let it go a long time ago.

A very successful friend of mine has received a chorus of unfair public attacks on his character. These attacks come from people who do not know him personally. Through some of the most violent assaults,

I have seen him consistently respond with dignity and character as he continues to forgive and grant mercy. As I watch how this wise man handles this, I ask myself how I am going to get to that place.

Because I, on the other hand, still have not forgiven the idiot who cut me off in traffic last week (evidenced by the fact that I just called him an idiot). I mean, come on, who does that? I drive a large SUV, and I could squash you. (See? The bitterness is still there.)

I always want mercy for myself, of course. I give that obligatory wave and smile when I cut you off in traffic, because of course when I do it it's an accident, but for you I want some straight up Old Testament, death match, fire-and-brimstone justice!

Forgiveness to a Whole Nutha Level

How do we get to the place where we can be merciful even to those who show us no mercy? How do we live out Jesus' command in our lives?

The first step is to admit our selfish desire for vengeance and call it what it is: sin. I don't want to spoil the ending for you, but we are going to be asked to do that a lot in this book.

As long as we make excuses for why we can't, won't, or just are not ready to forgive someone, we are just making excuses for continuing to sin. As we take this step we begin to move through several levels of forgiveness that are a part of the journey toward Christ-centered living.

The First Level of Forgiveness Is Easy

Let's be honest. If someone is willing to make amends, say they are sorry, agree to never do it again, and pay back emotionally and financially everything that they took from us, most of us can eke out a heartfelt "OK—I forgive you." Our forced smile hides the part that goes unsaid: "and by the way, I still do not trust you and never want to see you again. But I forgive you."

This level of forgiveness is horizontal and very me-istic. It is all about me. It's bottom-rung, low-hanging-fruit forgiveness. We can all grab it pretty easily and feel like we have done something. But it's very conditional, easy forgiveness, and puts the majority of the responsibility on the offending party.

The Second Level of Forgiveness Is a Little Harder

I think this is the level of forgiveness that most of us who call ourselves Christ-followers—including me—shoot for. This is when we are willing to have mostly unconditional (how's that for an oxymoron?) forgiveness for someone. As long as they stop hurting us and at least show some sort of remorse, we are willing to forgive them and may even upgrade them to "forgive *and* forget." We will see them in line at Starbucks and act friendly, or at family get-togethers we will hug.

This is a higher level of forgiveness and a very freeing place to be. I will be honest with you, though. This is sometimes a tough climb for me. I am a little scared of the altitude that this type of forgiveness takes me to, but it's worth it when the view gives us perspective from which we can see others in a new way . . . the way that God sees them. Although this would seem like we have crossed some good-enough line in God's economy, the truth is we are still short of God's will for our lives.

The Real Goal Is the Third Level of Forgiveness

Forgiveness to the third power—this is the wasabi-punch forgiveness that Jesus called *mercy*.

This is the highest level of forgiveness. It takes us to a whole new level and really a whole new dimension. On this level we start to see even more clearly from God's view—clear enough to see that we ourselves are in need of the mercy of the court, and clear enough to realize that the fault that we have held against someone is, well, small in comparison to the offense that we have made against God.

In Matthew 7, Jesus said that the person who refuses to forgive others is like a man shouting and pointing at a speck of sawdust in someone else's eye when he himself has a huge plank in his own eye. How often do we walk around with huge planks hanging out of our eyes, saying, "Hey buddy! Look at you! How can you live with yourself with that sawdust in your eyes? I cannot believe that you would walk around like that! You are unbelievable . . ."

You see the point.

Jesus told his disciples a parable in Matthew 18 about a plank-eyed guy. This guy, a servant, owed his master ten million dollars. The master ordered that the servant's entire family be sold and that he be thrown in jail until he could pay everything he owed. Jesus says, "The servant fell on his knees before him. 'Be patient with me,' he begged, 'and I will pay back everything.' The servant's master took pity on him, canceled the debt and let him go" (Matthew 18:26-27).

But then the guy leaves and goes out on a little victory lap through town and, lo and behold, he sees a man who owes him eleven bucks—a speck compared to the man's own log-like debt. "His fellow servant fell to his knees and begged him, 'Be patient with me, and I will pay you back'" (Matt 18:29). Sounds familiar doesn't it?

The man refused to grant the same mercy the master had shown him.

> Instead, he went off and had the man thrown into prison until he could pay the debt. When the other servants saw what had happened, they were greatly distressed and went and told their master everything that had happened. Then the master called the servant in. "You wicked servant," he said, "I canceled all that debt of yours because you begged me to. Shouldn't you have had mercy on your fellow servant just as I had on you?" In anger his master turned him over to the jailers to be tortured, until he should pay back all he owed. This is how my heavenly Father will treat each of you unless you forgive your brother from your heart.
>
> Matthew 18:30-35

Just like that servant, I want mercy for ME; I want justice for YOU.

So how do we attain this forgiveness to the third power? How do we go to this depth?

Real forgiveness goes beyond our three-dimensional world. We must go into an unseen dimension, where God's supernatural forgiveness toward us gives us the power to extend unending forgiveness to others. This is a forgiveness that takes being willing to actually live out the cliché and "let go and let God." Ed Young Jr., the senior and founding pastor of Fellowship Church, gave a great message that greatly influenced my thinking on this subject and gives a great basis for much of the following truth.

The first step is to . . .

Admit That Forgiveness Is a God Thing

Just say, "God, this whole forgiveness thing is from you. I've been greatly forgiven, and because I've been greatly forgiven, I want to greatly forgive others. I want to live out a whole different level of forgiveness. I don't know how to, God, but I want you to help me."

In John 20:22-23, Jesus had just risen from the dead. The disciples were locked in a little room, scared to death. About this time Jesus walks in, and the Bible says, "He breathed on them and said, 'Receive the Holy Spirit.'"

It is telling that the very next thing Jesus speaks about is the subject of forgiveness. "If you forgive anyone his sins, they are forgiven; if you do not forgive them, they are not forgiven" (John 20:23).

Some have read this passage and interpret it with an emphasis on the fact that Jesus was giving his followers a special power to go and forgive people of their sins (as if Jesus was giving them the equivalent of a spiritual "hall pass" that would give them the authority to forgive sins). The truth, however, is that Jesus was opening up to them the power of the Holy Spirit (just as we have access today) and with that access came the same ability that Jesus had to forgive people. Jesus was more concerned with his disciples' ability to forgive people than he was their authority to forgive people. That is because forgiveness is a God thing.

Jesus knew what it was that he had just taken care of on the cross. He had just done the work of forgiveness. His resurrection was evidence of this and his perfect life paid for this and his sacrifice wiped out all of our sins. If Jesus had a to-do list in front of him it would have looked like this.

Live perfect life (check)

Die on cross (check)

Rise again to show I am for real and defeat death (check)

Give disciples power of Holy Spirit (check)

Teach disciples about forgiving as well

Forgiveness is a God thing. So, we've got to allow him to do his thing. What we are saying is, "God, I don't feel like it. I don't want to do it. But I know forgiveness is who you are and you forgave me. God, help me forgive."

After we allow God to do his thing, which begins with letting him forgive us, then we have to . . .

Take Action and Do Our Part

God gives us the grace and the power through the Holy Spirit to do it, but it is our choice to live it out or not. The power is there. The mercy is there. We make the choice.

We serve an initiative-taking God. God is all about preemptive forgiveness. Jesus did the work on the cross and died for our sins before they were even committed. He did his part long before we even thought about doing our part. A favorite verse of mine is Romans 12:18, because it gives us such a clear understanding of our part in the forgiveness process:

"If it is possible, as far as it depends on you, live at peace with everyone."

As far as it depends on who? You. Live at peace with everyone. Our responsibility does not lie in how people react to our forgiveness, if they change their ways or even if they ever admit they were wrong. Our only responsibility is to offer mercy and peace. In giving these two important gifts, we become more like Jesus.

The third thing we have to do is . . .

Get Off the Emotional Roller Coaster

Our emotions lie to us and deceive us. We often become intoxicated by our anger, happiness, sadness, or other emotions and are left with an emotional hangover. In order to make sober decisions we must somehow separate ourselves from our emotions. I don't *feel* like forgiving people who hurt me. Do you? Am I the only one here? I just don't feel like it. But you know what? If I were to draw a line that says, "I'm not going to forgive until I feel like it," I would never forgive! Nor would you.

Our feelings are freaky-deaky. Feelings can't be trusted. But here's what I've learned about my own life: If I don't feel like forgiving, that's probably a good sign that I really need to forgive. Did you underline that and highlight it? If there is a spirit of unforgiveness in a situation, put horns on it and call it what it is—SIN.

In Galatians 5, Paul talks about the fruit of the Spirit. In other words, the moment Christ comes into our lives, the Holy Spirit plants seeds in us, and those seeds produce this supernatural fruit. Well, one of the fruits Paul talks about in Galatians 5 is self-control. Not emotions. Not feelings. Self-control.

Through parenting, my wife and I have learned that teaching our children to be able to control their emotions is one of the vital foundational building blocks of "raising a child in the way he or she should go," and that if not done can produce some pretty self-centered, out of control adults. You can see evidence of this on a simple walk through Walmart!

As parents we ask more questions and seek more advice on the issue of "self-control training" than any other issue, because it is so important to understand the havoc our emotions can wreak if left unchecked. When we have our emotions in check and our self under the control of the Holy Spirit we can take a vantage that is God's vantage, which allows us to forgive in a way that is beyond our normal abilities.

The last thing we do is to . . .

Trust God with Our Enemies

You're probably excited now. "Is he writing what I think he is writing? Shawn, are you saying what I think you're saying? God will have his way? YES! Do I get to decide the form of punishment?" Before you get too excited and start making a list of creative revenge tactics, look at Luke 6. Trusting God means giving complete control of the situation to him—letting our anger go and even—wait for it—praying for our enemies. Wasabi.

Do what?

In Luke 6:27-28, Christ says, "Love your enemies, do good to those who hate you, bless those who curse you, pray for those who mistreat you."

This stuff will mess us up, won't it?

It's a one-two wasabi punch, swimming completely against the current of who we are naturally. But it is what God wants for us—to be merciful, as we have been shown mercy.

When we look deeply at the act of mercy—of deep and true forgiveness—the miracle is not forgetting what someone has done to us. The miracle is remembering it and choosing to forgive and blessing those who have wronged us. Because when we remember it and choose to forgive, our memories can become memorials of the grace of God. We will no longer see these memorials with the remembrance of the offense, but rather see a memorial of all that God can do in our lives. And that just continues to free us up to be the kind of people that God desires.

TAKE A BITE

It's time to hold your nose and take a big bite of that wasabi.

So who is it for you? Who is that person or persons that you don't want to forgive, who don't deserve forgiveness and in fact you are not able to forgive? Hard as it is, that's the thing that God wants you to do. Like a punch to the gut, isn't it? Consider praying a prayer something like this:

God, I hate _____ and I want nothing to do with forgiving _____. Today I am admitting that this is sin. I am asking you to forgive me of this sin and as an act of worship toward you I am asking you to help me do the same for _____. Today I start the journey that ends with me being able to remember but choose to forgive. In an act of faith I will say: I love _____ because you love me.

June 2

Bitterness can really eat away at your soul--
like some parasite or rodent is gnawing on you
all day long. On some days, I'm not even sure
I have much of a soul left. I've been going to
this church long enough that I know all the
right things to say--that I should forgive my
dad and move on--and I think I even agree
with the things I say. But how do you let go
of something that has defined you for twenty
years? I don't even know who I'd be without
the bitterness. Sad and scary, isn't it?

When the things people have done to hurt you
play over and over in your brain like a never-
ending loop, it is really hard to forgive and
forget. As much as I struggle with forgiving
others, though, I have an even harder time

Laura's Story: Part Two

forgiving myself. If it's true that God knows each one of us intimately and personally, then that means that God knows intimately and personally every bad decision and horrible thing I've ever done. And I'm assuming God's memory is perfect, so is there a never-ending loop of my wonderful choices running through God's head at all times?

Because, truthfully, I've made a royal mess of my life—in fact, I'm pretty sure that if there's a bad decision to be made, then I've made it. I wish that I could blame it all on my dad, because that would make things easier, but that's not really the truth—because things got even worse when I was on my own.

After I finally made it through my teen years, I just took off. I thought, if I could just get far enough away, then I could start over and be different. I can't even tell you how many times since then I've picked up and left a town, a job, a relationship, whatever the problem happened to be at the time, trying once again to start from scratch. I've tried new jobs, new houses, even new husbands (yes, that's _husbands_, as in multiple). But here was the problem: I brought _me_ with me.

I brought the same old habits and the same old hang-ups. I was still searching for the same guy who would fill my emptiness, and I was still willing to hurt people to make sure that I got what I wanted.

I don't know why I assumed there'd be a new me waiting in the new place. You know, a shiny sparkly upgraded version of myself, clean and fresh and ready to conquer the world? Ah, isn't it funny how we can deceive ourselves?

Instead, a trail of relational carnage behind me reeks to high heaven. And my suspicion is that if God is anything like Christians claim (all-knowing and everything) then there's no way God hasn't smelled it. All the stuff I thought I left behind? It's all right there stinking up the place. How can I get rid of that?

The church my friend takes me to talks a lot about grace: grace this and grace that, and isn't God's grace so wonderful? But I have a hard time even figuring out what it means. And the little bit that I do understand seems too good to be true. If God's so good, then God couldn't possibly be willing to just forgive me for all of the mess I've made. Sometimes I feel like I hate myself, hate the person I've let myself become. I couldn't possibly be worthy of being forgiven. Sometimes deep down, I think I deserve any bad thing that comes my way.

A trail of failed jobs and failed marriages, four children who I can barely manage to care for, and to top it all off I owe everyone I know money.

It's obvious I need serious help. Yes, I know that I have blown it in a lot of ways and that I have absolutely no clue of how I could ever fix things. I am asking for help. I believe in God, and they say Jesus can forgive all the junk in my past, but why would he? I don't even think I deserve it, so why would some perfect deity? I'm honestly not even sure that Jesus can really do that. Can he really take a life so empty and lost and find some purpose for the rest of it?

I sure hope so.

CHAPTER TWO

Are You Sure You're Allowed to Do That?

Then Jesus said to her, "Your sins are forgiven."
Luke 7:48

Forgiveness is a hard thing to give to someone.

It's even harder to forgive yourself.

Arriving at the place where we can forgive others who have hurt us is a level of living that most of us only dream of. If we are able to forgive ourselves, we come to a place where we really believe that Jesus has the power to forgive just as he has claimed.

The Bible does not give us a lot of her story, but we can probably all relate to her in one way or another. She was carrying around a lot of hurt, a lot of pain, and a ton of baggage. With what the Bible does give us, though, we know that life had not treated her well. By the time we meet her and find her in coming to Jesus she is at the end of what seems to be a very difficult journey towards forgiveness. Luke recounts the story like this:

> Now one of the Pharisees invited Jesus to have dinner with him, so he went to the Pharisee's house and reclined at the table. When a woman who had lived a sinful life in that town learned that Jesus was eating at the Pharisee's house, she brought an alabaster jar of perfume, and as she stood behind him at his feet weeping, she began to wet his feet with her tears. Then she wiped them with her hair, kissed them and poured perfume on them.
>
> *Luke 7:36-38*

The "sinful woman," as she is called by many scholars (as if there are non-sinful women or men), is a woman whose sins are apparent. Luke knew of her sin. The men around the table, especially the religious people, knew who she was. Religious people are sometimes the hardest on the people most broken and bruised by sin—the people most in need of God's love and grace. We have a tendency to be unlike Jesus toward "sinful people."

The Bible does not tell us exactly what made her such a "sinful" woman, but we can probably assume that she did not sin alone. Most people don't. Think through the list of sins that we are most offended by as religious people and you will find that there is a whole lot of sinnin' by a whole lot of people going on. Often the people who are the hardest on the sinners are a part of the sin or at least struggle with temptation in that area as well.

Because of the expense of the perfume she would anoint Jesus with, we can conclude that this woman made a lot of money on her "sinful life." She came in with all she had to offer, expensive perfume bought with dirty money and a sinful, yet repentant, heart.

We know from this scripture how the religious people thought of this woman, but I cannot help thinking of how she must have felt about herself. She was used to the stares, but I imagine that on this day she could feel the stares darting through her soul as she walked toward Jesus. These men, some of whom may have been clients, were waiting to see what she was up to and what she was doing here. Not only were women not allowed in this room, but certainly not *this* woman. Then she did it—something that Jesus would choose to teach us with, something that would live forever in God's word. She knelt down at his feet and gave attention to a man in a way that she had never done before. She was worshiping him because she knew that she needed something he was offering—forgiveness.

All of her life she had given attention to men for their pleasure and their needs, but this time she has a need. She had heard so much about this man, perhaps even that he is God. People are calling him the messiah, the savior, and saying that he has healed the sick and raised the dead. Some are even saying that he offers forgiveness of sin. She is nervous as she waits for his words.

What will he say to her?

How will he react?

Would Jesus kick her out of the house?

Will he call her names, or even have her dragged out into the street and stoned?

Some days, she has thought she should be stoned.

But he did something unexpected, something that neither the woman nor the Pharisees expected.

Jesus often does the unexpected.

He forgave her.

And people freaked out.

This guy was not allowed to do this. Forgive sins. You know, all of his great teachings were fine and they were even willing to give him a chance over dinner, but this was too far. For one thing, this woman did not deserve to be forgiven, but "Your sins are forgiven" are four words that rocked the room and rocked the world. It was a dropkick right to the spiritual gut of a bunch of Pharisees just like me. Probably just like you too.

And This Is a Problem Because . . . ?

I am not convinced that these men were against forgiveness.

In fact, most people I meet are for forgiveness.

Often when we read or talk about the Pharisees, we hear that they were more about condemnation than forgiveness, but I am not sure that was the case. The entire religious system that these men were a part of was all about forgiveness. It was just forgiveness through legalism, religiosity, works, and sacrifice. The problem here was not that they did not believe in the idea of forgiveness—they just did not believe that *Jesus* could forgive.

That is where the real rub comes in. They wanted to catch Jesus in this blasphemous lie that he could forgive sins. They wanted to expose him for the crazy person that he must have been. If these men had believed Jesus could actually forgive sins, there would have been a celebration. They probably would have insisted that well-known sinners like this woman be brought to Jesus to be forgiven. In fact, I think they would have been running through the city finding everyone they knew and having them come and be forgiven too. Most importantly, they would have been at his feet worshiping as well, rather than asking, "Jesus, are you sure you are allowed to do this?"

I know many of you would say, "dirty, rotten Pharisees." I am tempted to say the same thing. But then I remember that I would probably be right there with them. I would be a "dirty, rotten Pharisee," scoffing at Jesus' supposed divine power. You probably would be too. You might be quick to deny it, but let's think about this: sometimes when you really see the facts in front of you (like calling sushi dead raw fish) they start to look a lot different.

Fact one: A guy shows up on the scene saying he is God.
Fact two: Said guy says that he can heal people.
Fact three: The word on the street from his followers is that he can calm the sea, can walk on water, and has been known to turn water into wine.
Fact four: (Here is the doozie.) He says that he is God and can forgive sins.

Now given these facts that we cannot see, are you telling me that you would be a follower? When you look at it on paper, he sounds a little like David Koresh to me.

I think we cut ourselves a lot of slack that we do not offer to the Pharisees. These guys were living with these facts. These facts were staring them right in the face, apparent to no one more than Simon, the man who had invited Jesus over to his house.

Have you ever invited a new person into a group and been a little worried about the impression the person would make? It puts you on edge, wondering what the newbie might say or do that could make you the butt of jokes for some time to come. Usually they are just benign situations that we find ourselves laughing about later, but this was no laughing matter. This was a big deal. This was a big risk that Simon was taking.

> When the Pharisee who had invited him saw this, he said to himself, "If this man were a prophet, he would know who is touching him and what kind of woman she is—that she is a sinner."
>
> Luke 7:39

I imagine that Simon's stomach dropped a little. He was a Pharisee. In our culture we now equate that with "evil," but substitute "pastor" for "Pharisee," and you can begin to understand the regard most people would have had for these religious leaders. As a deeply religious man, Simon surely wanted the messiah to come. He needed the messiah to come. Jesus had come into the picture and now Simon was hoping that Jesus would prove to be the man—the God—that he was longing for. Then he saw that Jesus was not even aware of the sinful woman that was before him. His heart sank.

Yes, Even She Can Be Forgiven

Jesus saw into Simon's heart and I think he saw that disappointment and saw the heart of someone who he could teach. It was a moment, a window that presented itself—Jesus always took those moments.

I have had these types of moments with my daughter. I put her to bed every night. It is a part of our ritual that we say prayers as a family and then her mama turns off the light and I tuck her in and we talk. Most of the time this means that I tell her a story about a princess or we review the day, and sometimes we just tickle and giggle.

Then sometimes there is a window. A friend of mine encourages me to look for what he calls "windows to the heart." They don't come very often, but every now and then my daughter, even at three years old, will give me a glimpse into her soul, and I have an opportunity not just to talk but to listen to her heart and then teach. I spend my life waiting for these opportunities with her.

Jesus saw this opportunity with Simon.

> Jesus answered him, "Simon, I have something to tell you."
> "Tell me, teacher," he said.
> "Two men owed money to a certain moneylender. One owed him five hundred denarii, and the other fifty. Neither of them had the money to pay him back, so he canceled the debts of both. Now which of them will love him more?"
> Simon replied, "I suppose the one who had the bigger debt canceled."
> "You have judged correctly," Jesus said.
>
> *Luke 7:40-43*

Jesus chose to teach with a story. I love this story. Most of us can take a little sympathy on people who owe a great deal because we ourselves have been in a situation where we felt as if we owed more than we could ever repay. Most of us have also been in a situation where we could not pay (even if it was just a matter of not having enough change at the grocery check-out) and someone said, "Don't worry—I got it. Your debt is paid." We know the feeling of relief and freedom that comes with that moment.

I remember a moment like this for me while I was in seminary. I was working two part-time jobs and attending classes full-time, plus taking an additional two classes a semester to try and finish early. My wife was working five (and sometimes six) days a week in a good job, so we were making ends meet and even had a little to spend on ourselves, until the seminary bill arrived. Somehow, I had blocked it out of my mind that I would have to pay for all of the full-time tuition *plus* the fees for all of these extra classes that I was taking. And all of this would be due before I could register again. It was too much. There was really no way I could take an additional job on, there was just not enough time in the day, and the same was so for my wife as well. It was frustrating to know that no matter how hard we had worked at making this happen and no matter how hard we worked over the next month that it would never be enough.

My dad called out of the blue that week, and I just mentioned our predicament and that I really wanted to be able to continue with classes but that it looked like I would probably need to drop classes for a semester to be able to pay the bill. A few days later I received a hand-scribbled note that read "Remember your debt is canceled and so is your seminary bill" along with a check to pay off my account. I was elated. I was joyous. I felt a freedom because my huge, insurmountable debt had been paid.

Simon knew this feeling as well. At some point in his life he had been forgiven and he knew that the more you are forgiven for, the better you feel.

Then he [Jesus] turned toward the woman and said to Simon, "Do you see this woman? I came into your house. You did not give me any water for my feet, but she wet my feet with her tears and wiped them with her hair. You did not give me a kiss, but this woman, from the time I entered, has not stopped kissing my feet. You did not put oil on my head, but she has poured perfume on my feet. Therefore, I tell you, her many sins have been forgiven—for she loved much. But he who has been forgiven little loves little."

Then Jesus said to her, "Your sins are forgiven."

Luke 7:44-48

This is where Jesus throws down the big stuff.

He looks at Simon (and in doing so he is talking to all of the religious people gathered there in his house) and by a simple question makes one of the most telling statements in this passage.

"Do you see this woman?"

It's a simple question, really, that should have a simple answer. Either Jesus was being coy with Simon or he was trying to make a point. Knowing that Jesus obviously knew he could see this person right in front of him, Simon may have actually been tempted to respond, "Yes, Jesus. The question is do YOU see her?"

This is where we really have a contrast between what we believe about forgiveness and what Jesus believes.

Here is what Jesus was asking Simon.

When you walk through the city on the way to worship, do you see this woman?

When she is sad and quickly exiting the house of a client in the dark of the night, do you see her? Do you even know that she exists? Do you even know that she is real and hurting? Do you even see that *she* is one I came for?

Most of all, when you look across your house at her, do you see her like I do, as one who has come begging for forgiveness? One who knows whose presence she is in and one who knows that she should bring all that she has to offer—even if no one ever sees her.

Punch one.

Then he looks at the "sinful woman" in front of all of Simon's friends and says the words that none of them would ever forget (especially her), "Your sins are forgiven."

Punch two.

Jesus forgave someone that the others had been unable to forgive.

Jesus forgave a woman who had been unable to forgive herself.

Jesus forgave on behalf of God.

> The other guests began to say among themselves, "Who is this who even forgives sins?"
> Jesus said to the woman, "Your faith has saved you; go in peace."
> Luke 7:49-50

Who are you in this story?

Some Still Need Forgiveness

The truth is that the bell just rang and life has eaten your lunch. You are hungry for something, or someone who can give you an ounce of hope. You have gathered up all you have—which is not much—and you have brought it to Jesus' feet in hopes that he will accept it as an offering. Here is the good news. He does.

When I was in the eleventh grade, Jesus saved me and changed my entire life. Over the next few months I witnessed to anyone who moved and invited everyone I could to a group I had started on campus called "Teens for Christ." I had really lost track of whom I had invited and most importantly (or annoyingly) how many times I had invited them.

One afternoon in the hallway I saw a girl who I knew carried a good bit of hurt on her face and covered it up with a crazy, fun personality. But I could tell she was longing for something more, or at least I thought she was. So I asked her if she would come to "Teens for Christ." Apparently I had asked before and she was a little annoyed. She said, "I'm not coming to your 'Teens for Christ' meeting, dear sir. I will be unable to attend." (That is the censored version for when her daughter reads this later.) You can guess what she may have screamed at me. I thought all was lost and quite frankly, as a little bit of a legalistic zealot, I figured she could clean that mouth up in hell as that would be where she would be one day, and moved onto my next invite.

Then about one month later I was a little freaked out when I saw this same girl walking towards me in tears at a Fellowship of Christian Athletes meeting. She walked up to me and said that she had noticed a difference in my life and that she wanted that difference too. I walked her through the gospel and prayed with her and Jesus saved her that night. It was Monday, September 16, 1991. You may be asking how I remember that date so well. It's because exactly four years and three months later, I would marry that foul-mouthed girl (she has since cleaned up her act a lot) and we would spend the rest of our lives together.

To me the best thing about my wife's story is that she knew that she needed forgiveness. She was like all of us have been at some point in our lives. The difference is, she was also willing to accept it. So many times I know that I am so oblivious to my own sin and my own failings that I don't even know that I need to sit at Jesus' feet and allow him to forgive me.

She knew that she needed someone to show her toward this person named Jesus, and she found a group of people that she had heard knew him and showed up at their house. Then she brought all that she had, which was almost nothing except baggage and hurt, and brought it to Jesus as a young sixteen-year-old girl. She knew she needed to believe that Jesus could really forgive her.

Do you believe that Jesus can really forgive you? Or have you gotten so desensitized to the sin and hurt in your life that you are like the hundreds of "sinful women" who did not come to see Jesus at Simon's house that day?

When will you say "enough hurt"? When will you say "enough doubt"? When will you say "enough self-punishment"? When will be your day that you will remember like my wife and I both remember September 16, 1991? Today? Will today be the day that you finally let go and let God change your life and offer you the forgiveness that he offered that woman that day? I hope it will be.

Some Need to Believe That Jesus Can Forgive

Then some of us are more like Simon. You are OK with the theology and the idea of forgiveness, and you may even be OK with God forgiving some of the better people of the world because of all they have done, but when it comes to the people who really need forgiveness, you don't really believe that God can forgive. You and I would have been sitting right alongside the Pharisees in this story, saying, "Who is this who even forgives sins?"

I think it is because we don't really understand love. Not just any love, but a transforming love that rocks us to our core and we cannot even begin to understand. This is a love that caused Jesus to climb onto a cross for our sins, and yet we somehow think that after that raw demonstration of love, he would hold back his forgiveness from us and not offer the fullest of freedom. This kind of forgiveness takes love.

> For God so loved the world that he gave his one and only Son, that whoever believes in him shall not perish but have eternal life. For God did not send his Son into the world to condemn the world, but to save the world through him.
>
> John 3:16-17

I try not to be cliché. It's hard for me, because clichés really make sense to me. I think that is why they make the cut as clichés. "God is love" has become a bit of a cliché, and yet they may be the three most powerful words in the world. And to boot it's direct from scripture.

> God is love.
> 1 John 4:8, 16

It is hard to really wrap our arms around this statement. I think that is why we do not understand forgiveness. Think about it with me just a little.

If we really believe that God is love and that in this love he crawled out of heaven and then onto a tree to die for the sin we committed and the sin that he did not . . .

If we believe that this death was for one reason—and one reason only—to forgive the debt of our sin, and most of all that in this death Jesus gave everything for us . . .

And if we believe that God let his son die for us so that he could offer us that forgiveness, then why is it that we do not believe it is truly available? I mean we think it's available if you are teetering right along the good-enough line, but if you are really in need of forgiveness we somehow think that God has given up and said, "well I paid for everything—just not that!"

> God made him who had no sin to be sin for us, so that in him we might become the righteousness of God.
>
> 2 Corinthians 5:21

Jesus Saved You

Jesus (who had no sin) saved me (who had a lot of sin). Over the last few years, I have made an intentional change in the way that I describe my salvation experience. I used to say "I accepted Christ" on January 26, 1991. I have come to realize that was an error. I now say, "Jesus saved me" on January 26, 1991. I know that this may seem like a small nuance and nothing more than semantics, but to me it is the key to this whole forgiveness thing because Jesus is the only actor in the one-man act that is the story of our salvation. We all try our best to sneak in a cameo appearance—but our actions have nothing to do with our salvation.

When you are tempted to not forgive others, and more importantly, when you are not willing to forgive yourself, remember that *Jesus saved you.*

He chose to forgive me. Who am I to withhold that forgiveness from others?

He chose to forgive you. Who are you to not forgive yourself?

TAKE A BITE

How long are you going to hang onto the guilt? How long will you punish yourself or someone else? Isn't it time you believe what Jesus said when he forgave you? I know that it's impossible to believe but God chose to love you knowing everything about you, even the stuff you're hanging onto. God chose you. Say that to yourself, "God chose me." And God forgave you too.

Jesus, thank you for forgiving me. Thank you that even when you knew every detail of my life you chose to say four simple words, "I forgive your sins." I accept those words in my life today and I believe that you are allowed to forgive me because you are God. Heal me and forgive me.

June 15

I'm usually a pretty tolerant person. Don't get me wrong, I get annoyed with any and everyone and have a tendency to snap at people when I think they're being idiots (and in my humble opinion, this describes most people most of the time). But I know that with where I've been and what I've done in my life, I can't go about judging other people for the things they do. People have a right to act however they want, don't you think? And I can either accept it and move on, or waste unnecessary energy that could be better spent elsewhere.

With that being said, I have to confess this: there is a woman at work that I truly hate. Marilyn. And when I say I hate her, I don't just mean that I don't like her. I literally mean that when I think of her, anger starts boiling up in the pit of my stomach, running through my veins, tying my chest up in knots until it's all I can do not to explode or turn into the Hulk or something. I want to hurt her. I want to destroy her. I want to wipe the memory of her off the face of the earth. I want . . . Well now I'm just getting worked up. Rein it in, Laura.

I know I just went through all that stuff about forgiving my father for the things he did to me when I was young. But what do you do when someone is continually doing bad things to you? An onslaught of horrible things everyday? I'm pretty sure Marilyn spends her time trying to think of new ways to hurt me and bring me down and ruin my reputation.

You see, it all started last month when I was promoted and she wasn't. Man, can women ever be catty. I'm convinced that if we ever decided to just support one another instead of trying to hold one another back all the time, we'd pretty much be able to run the world. But I digress. So I get the job, she doesn't, and she decides to make it her personal mission to make my life as miserable as possible.

It started small enough with those passive-aggressive comments that we all know and love. But then she started spreading it around that my kids all have different fathers, and what that means about me. Even worse, what that means about my kids. Then she started making up things about me to tell the boss—that I was rude to some customers, that I didn't do my job right, that I was inappropriate with a coworker. And for some reason lately, whenever it's been my turn to close out the registers, we turn up short, making it look like I'm stealing! This woman is toxic with a capital T. Now, even some of our other coworkers are acting differently around me, suddenly stopping their conversation when I walk in the room, giving each other knowing looks when my kids are around. And you want to know the worst part? I saw her at the church my friend Anne has been dragging me to. That made my blood boil. Aren't Christians supposed to be better people than the rest of us? It just made me hate her all the more.

I spotted her at the coffee station in the lobby before worship started, and stopped dead in my tracks. Anne asked what was wrong, and I told her who the woman was and all the bad things she'd done to me. Anne was very sympathetic (and who wouldn't be? I'm clearly the innocent here, being attacked by a truly malicious, evil person). But then Anne surprised me.

She suggested I pray for Marilyn.

Are you insane? God knows what an awful person Marilyn is. I'm the one that needs praying for! Pray that I don't get fired for the stuff she's falsely accusing me of. Pray that Marilyn moves to Timbuktu and all this gossip about me ends. Pray that I don't smack her straight in the face (or worse!) next time I see her!

I said all this to Anne, but she just said that Marilyn might have some major issues of her own that make her act the way she does, and even if she doesn't and really is just a cruel, heartless person, it will help the situation if I could try to love Marilyn.

Hang on a second. Love her? Can't we just start with liking her, even? She's my enemy--hating her is kind of part of the deal. On the other hand, hating her hasn't made the situation any better, and it certainly hasn't made _me_ feel any better. I could try to pray for her--to love her--but how?

CHAPTER THREE

I Have to Love Osama Too?

You have heard that it was said, "Love your neighbor and hate your enemy." But I tell you: Love your enemies and pray for those who persecute you.
Matthew 5:43-44

One of the difficult things with Jesus is that he is so incredibly consistent. He came to die for people who sinned, and the Bible is pretty clear that everyone has sinned. Now, I was never real sharp in arithmetic, but I can run that little equation to its logical end and know that it means he came to die for everyone. Not just for good, white-bread Americans, but also for all of our—wait for it—enemies.

Now, so far in this book we have talked about forgiving people who hurt us and Jesus' audacious claim to be able to forgive sins.

Those statements of Jesus got up in my chili a little (I hope they did yours too), but this one in Matthew 5:43-48 is straight-up crazy talk. Not at first glance, mind you. Love and prayer are both very good sounding things that we like to hear Jesus talk about. It's the "who" we are to love and pray for that is the kind of talk that got Jesus in trouble. This is the stuff that got him killed. This is the stuff that would get him hated and probably killed by Christians today too.

As a Christian—and I hesitate to use that word since I often don't act like a Christ-follower—I sure have some hate issues. I can say that with certainty, given the fact that some of the worst hate crimes in our world are committed in Jesus' name.

It seems that in our world, even more so than in Jesus' time on earth, the truth will get you some hate mail.

As I am writing this book, we have just come out of a presidential election season. As I watched the folks debate and posture and then spin and posture some more, I have come to realize that you almost cannot survive in politics if you tell the absolute truth. I know a few folks who have, and it seems to make life as a politician incredibly hard for them.

As I see what it takes to get 51 percent or so of the people to vote for you so you can represent 100 percent of the people, it becomes painfully obvious why Jesus said that the gate that leads to being elected by him is so narrow. I mean, you start talking like this and people are just not going to go for it.

There were several instances in the Bible where Jesus spoke to a crowd or maybe even an individual and his words caused them to walk away. One such example involves a story we will look at in more depth in a later chapter. Jesus has an encounter with a young, hip, and rich dude who sincerely wanted to follow Jesus. Jesus goes right after a character issue in his heart. It was not to humiliate him, but rather because he loved him that he sees into the young man's heart and says these words:

> *"One thing you lack," he said. "Go, sell everything you have and give to the poor, and you will have treasure in heaven. Then come, follow me."*
> *At this the man's face fell. He went away sad, because he had great wealth.*
>
> *Mark 10:21-22*

What stands out to me here is the reaction an individual who really loved God had to the honest and transparent words of someone who was sharing truth. His face fell. He went away sad.

I have a feeling that a lot of people's faces will fall and they will go away sad when they come to realize that the commands of Jesus do not line up at all with our "get even and win at all costs" approach to life in our world today.

There Are Enemies, and Then There Are Enemies

Jesus' wasabi-punch here is that if we really want to look like our father, and truly have his DNA, we will love our enemies as much as we love our friends. As Jesus points out, it is pretty easy to love those who love you back. The real test of love like our father's is when we love those who hate us—those Jesus called our enemies.

Now on first blush, this is not too bad because we have two types of enemies in our minds. We have those who are our enemies because of a petty feud or some hurt in our lives and we have declared a small war on them, but we assume that at some point a truce will be called and we'll move on with life. These are small-time enemies.

Then we have the other enemies. Our "real" enemies. These are the people who stand against our country, our family, and our religion in such a way that they literally are a threat to our way of life. These are the enemies that make us fearful and angry to the point we truly believe that . . .

- If the other political party were to have its way with our tax system or were to influence the solutions to the social issues we hold dear, it would threaten our life and the lives of people we love.

- If the other race or nation is able to continue their way of dealing with our race or nation, we would see our rights and our privileges taken away or changed in major ways.

- If the other religion has its way, it would proselytize and recruit new followers and change our communities in an attempt to eradicate our religion and see its own radical agenda advanced.

As we size up these parties, races, nations, and religions, we often allow fear of people and fear of hurt to our way of life to cause us to become very unchristian. Can you see where this line of thinking would cause pain in our lives and would most certainly not be the way of Jesus?

To hate a group, or individual for that matter, stirs up feelings in our heart that expose the very base nature of our sinful soul.

OK, you and I say. But it's still OK to hate some people, right?

> *You have heard that it was said, "Love your neighbor and hate your enemy." But I tell you: Love your enemies and pray for those who persecute you, that you may be sons of your Father in heaven. He causes his sun to rise on the evil and the good, and sends rain on the righteous and the unrighteous. If you love those who love you, what reward will you get? Are not even the tax collectors doing that? And if you greet only your brothers, what are you doing more than others? Do not even pagans do that? Be perfect, therefore, as your heavenly Father is perfect.*
>
> *Matthew 5:43-48*

As I read Matthew 5:43-48, the first people who jump to my mind are Adolf Hitler and Osama bin Laden. You know, the people it's "OK" to hate, the really nasty people that make us feel like our sin is kindergarten level and we can get a little "wink, wink" from God for cheating on our taxes because it's not like we killed thousands of people or anything.

So, to illustrate how crazy this Jesus guy really was, let's use Osama for a little experiment. If Jesus was teaching in twenty-first-century America, I wonder if he might have said it like this.

> *You have heard that it was said, "Love your North American, European allies and Judeo-Christian counterparts and hate your Muslim terrorist enemies." But I tell you: Love terrorists and pray for those who hate and hurt you, that you may have the same DNA of your Father in heaven. He causes his sun to rise on Osama bin Laden and on the people of America, and sends rain on both the mosque and the church down the street. If you love your friends and those who agree with you, what reward will you get? Are not even the terrorists doing that? And if you say good things only about your own country, what are you doing more than the people who hate you in the Middle East? Do not even the terrorists do that? Be perfect just like your Father is perfect.*
>
> *Shawn's not-so-perfect interpretation of Matthew 5:43-48*

Now that just is not what I want to hear. If I were to truly be honest with you, I have a terrible time loving Clemson Tiger fans (the rival for my beloved Gamecocks), much less the guy who seeks to kill everyone like me in the world including my wife and children.

But what are you saying, Jesus, is that I have to love Osama too?

Jesus Blows the Curve

For some reason we have developed a "grade on a curve" theology when it comes to sin. The problem is that Jesus just blows that curve worse than Einstein in a physics 101 class.

I will never forget one time in college when I definitely lost the Mr. Congeniality contest. During my senior year, I took a class on systematic theology, which is great for religion majors like me, but is quite a mistake for people who unwittingly decided to take the class as their religion elective. This was one of those classes that really causes stress because we basically had a few "quizzes" based on hundreds of pages of reading, and one final exam. The quizzes were weighted rather low at 20 percent of the overall grade, and the final counted for 80 percent.

I enjoyed the reading (yeah, I know, I am a nerd) so I had done pretty well on the quizzes (all 100s, so long as we're being transparent and humble). I am an auditory learner as well, so when the prof announced that the final exam would be taken entirely from his lectures, I was a happy man. I have a pretty good memory, so this was looking like a pretty easy couple of nights for me. The best part of this entire scenario to me was that I always loved it when my roommate had to pull all-nighters and I could go play ping-pong—yes I am that deep.

As we neared the end of the class and approached the final exam, my professor decided to let everyone know that he would be grading the final exam on a curve. In other words, the highest grade would be rounded up to 100, and every grade below that would be increased the same number of points. If you have ever been struggling in a class, you know that is music to a struggling student's ears. The exam came and went, and on the last day of class, the professor handed out our graded exams. He started the class by announcing, "We have some of you who really need the curve on this one, and I have some good news for you. The second highest grade is an 87." Everyone immediately started doing calculations in their brains and figuring out what score, plus 13, would give them the grade they needed. Then the professor continued, "but I also have some bad news. One of you made a 100." The wind came out of the room. I sat and prayed for the first time in my life for an 87. Apparently I had prayed more for the 100 a few days earlier. Yep. It was me. I blew the curve and everyone hated me just a little for it.

I guess it is this belief that Jesus grades on a curve that makes us think that we can legitimately have enemies. We all have figured out pretty easily that we are not making a 100 percent . . . I mean, "all have fallen short," and we have accepted that. But we also know that there are some zeros out there too— Hitler, bin Laden, Stalin, the guy who invented e-mail spam. You know, the really egregious sinners. We know we're better than those guys.

We also know that we are better than most people—especially that neighbor who never cuts his grass—so we assume that we are somewhere in that sweet safe zone that is at least a B if not an A-. We like that.

But then comes Jesus.

Yep, he scored a 100. Perfect. Not in the "I was a nerd with a fairly good memory so I got 100 percent in one class and now am including that in a book" perfect, but the real-deal perfect.

The curve is blown.

And here is the truth—the only grade that passes is 100. So we just got put in the same boat as the guy who invented spam (and all the aforementioned mass-murderers). That is so not cool.

It is with this context now that we reread our wasabi scripture and see that Jesus is giving us a one-two-three punch to the gut in regards to the standard of love that he has asked us to hold.

First Punch, a Change in Thinking

You have heard that it was said, "Love your neighbor and hate your enemy."
Matthew 5:43

Have you ever gone a long period of time under the impression that you had correct information only to find that you have been running in the wrong direction? Some of you may be thinking of really small things, like the name of the guy five cubicles down from you (like when you have been calling him Bob for so long and then one day someone says, "dude, his name is Bill") or maybe it was some bad directions that took you off course for a few miles until you realized you were headed in the wrong direction (or ended up in another state).

For me, it was just a few years after I became a Christ-follower. I was a junior in college, and I had a great friend who was African American, but I can honestly say that I really did not care what color he was—he was just a friend. It was the farthest thing from my mind. I really had not even thought about the fact that he was a different race, well, until one day in the lunchroom. We were all there, eating our fifth bowl of Captain Crunch, when my friend walked into the cafeteria toward my table and kissed his girlfriend a quick good-bye.

Why would a kiss of a girlfriend bother me, you ask? Great question.

Because that girlfriend was white.

It seemed I had dealt with every issue that had marred my life prior to accepting Christ, except apparently this one. At the age of twenty, I was shown by the Holy Spirit that I was a racist.

I grew up in a very small, rural town that was deeply divided by race. As I have matured as a Christ-follower, I have realized that there was a level of racism that was "just accepted" in my town, school, and perhaps even among some of my family members. I realized that there was a casual, yet very present "hate" of anyone who was unlike me in race, creed, or social status. I would have never called it hate, but as my heart was being exposed, I realized my soul still had some very dark parts.

It is a humbling experience when your soul is exposed for who you really are.

When I was seventeen years old, Jesus chose to save me and just like he always does, he saved all of me—even the dirty, lousy, racist parts.

I went from being that guy who prided himself in having some "black friends" to just having friends. I went from being a guy who made excuses for some of the travesties that people in our country have committed against people of other races because it was "all they knew," to being appalled. I went from being a boy who thought it was "just the way it is" to a man who realizes that it can be so much better. God really did change my heart. But all of a sudden I realized that although Jesus had indeed saved me from my sin, I was drawn back to it with my reaction to that kiss.

You see, I had allowed a lie that had been sold to me as a young man to live as a truth in my heart.

This is what Jesus was warning against in this first statement. Don't believe the lie that says it's OK to love your friends and those you find easy to love, but hate those who are different from you or whom you don't really know. Jesus is turning the conventional wisdom on its head. Boom. Punch to the gut one.

Second Punch, a Whole Nutha Level

But I tell you: Love your enemies and pray for those who persecute you, that you may be sons of your Father in heaven.

Matthew 5:44-45

After exposing the lie, Jesus points out to us that we need to get spiritual with this issue. Jesus knew that we can all ignore our enemies. We can even get to a point where we are truly not

wishing them harm even—but to pray for them? To actually pe-
tition our father with the treasure that is prayer—our commu-
nication with God—and use this for our enemies, now that is a
huge step. Jesus taught us elsewhere in Matthew in relation to
money that "where your treasure is, there your heart will be also"
(6:21). This principle is true here as well. Jesus knows that when
we make the commitment to pray for our enemies, they will become treasures to us and where our treasures are, our heart will
follow. As we pray for our enemies, Jesus knew we would grow
to love them too. This is another level. This is the act of becoming
like our father. This is becoming a Christ-follower and not just a
feelings follower. This changes our heart.

And our hearts are really the subject at hand. The only reason for
all of this is that our hearts will beat more like our Father's—and
in turn more like Jesus'. Jesus' goal in this teaching is not about
our comfort, or even our lack of comfort. It's not about feeling
warm and fuzzy, and it is not even about our enemies (because
the truth is that they are sinners too in need of a heart change).
The bottom line is that Jesus is in constant pursuit of the transformation of our hearts, and he knows that the hatred of our enemies is a heart disease that can ruin that transformation.

Third Punch, There Is No Curve

He causes his sun to rise on the evil and the good, and sends rain on
the righteous and the unrighteous. If you love those who love you, what
reward will you get? Are not even the tax collectors doing that? And if
you greet only your brothers, what are you doing more than others? Do
not even pagans do that? Be perfect, therefore, as your heavenly Father
is perfect.

Matthew 5:45-48

There really is no curve when it comes to sin. Somewhere in this world, there is someone we have hurt in such a way, no matter how small we may think it is, that we have become a terrorist to their heart and in turn an enemy to them. We have all fallen short. We have all sinned, and we are all enemies of God until we allow God to save us and hand us the rights of Jesus.

So how do we do this? What are some principles that we can enact in our lives to help us love even our enemies in this way? There is a passage in the Old Testament that gives us some of the most concise and simple (notice I did not say easy) description of what it would mean to look like Jesus.

> *He has showed you, O man, what is good.*
> *And what does the LORD require of you?*
> *To act justly and to love mercy*
> *and to walk humbly with your God.*
> *Micah 6:8*

As I read these words from more than 2700 years ago, I am drawn to the question, "what does the LORD require of you?" These are marching orders that our God has sent that if we will follow them will change us and make us more like God.

God's first requirement is for us to "act justly." This means to do what is right and fair, not just what is best for us or easy. All of us have power over someone, even if it is simply the power to hate within our hearts (a private power, but massive power all the same). This power has brought many Christ-followers to their shame. What God is requiring here is that we know this power and the temptations it can bring and calling us to resist them. To "act justly" does not mean just to do good in the sight of others, but to live a life of integrity with a passion to treat those we hate justly.

Next we are asked to "love mercy." Greg Surratt, my pastor, says that we like to switch these two and love justice and act mercifully. This second command is not just to show mercy but to make it your passion. *Mercy* is that crazy word that we talked about in chapter 1 where we defy all of the logic of our hearts and actually forgive and love those who seek to hurt us. Even those who continue to hurt us. Especially those who continue to hurt us. This is not easy stuff. This is the stuff that Christ-followers are made of and the stuff that lives are changed by. There is a deep longing and a deep yearning for this type of love that exists in us all because God put it there. Mercy is a crazy love. The opening monologue of the 2003 movie *Love Actually* puts it wonderfully:

> *Whenever I get gloomy with the state of the world I think about the arrivals gate at Heathrow Airport. General opinion is starting to make out that we live in a world of hatred and greed. I don't see that. It seems to me that love is everywhere. . . . Fathers and sons, mothers and daughters, husbands and wives. . . . When the planes hit the twin towers none of the phone calls from the people on board were messages of hate or revenge. They were all messages of love.*

When we love mercy we are sending messages of love.

The third requirement calls us to "walk humbly with your God." In order to sustain this justice and mercy that we begin to offer, we have to walk in humility in constant relationship with God. This is a daily walk that leaves behind pride. Pride can take over our lives and destroy us. Pride can convince us we are worthy of God's love and forgiveness and that our enemies are not. Humility can help us walk with God and gives God the opportunity to help us take each step. Scripture says, "Humble yourselves before the Lord, and he will lift you up" (James 4:10).

As we really examine our hearts as it pertains to our enemies—those whom we think are somehow less deserving of God's love and mercy than us, but more deserving of God's justice—we have to admit that the love Jesus calls us to does not come naturally. As people of God, we are to act in a way that may be contrary to our hearts, to act in a way we may not even feel. It is easy to love our neighbors and friends, but Jesus calls us to a whole nutha level of love.

As simple and benign as we like to make Jesus' words, this is a serious shock to our system. The world and often even the church teach us to categorize people as either friends or enemies—as those we should love or those it's OK not to love.

But to love our enemies is counter to our feelings and counter to our culture. Jesus socks us right between the eyes with a command so terrifying and yet so powerful that if we really obey, we can turn the world upside down.

TAKE A BITE

So who are your enemies? You know, the group that you want to love justice with instead of acting mercifully? The group that even thinking about praying for them or loving them turns your stomach a little? God wants you to forgive them. God wants you not only to forgive them but to pray for them. God also wants us to pray for them. It's that simple—not easy, but it's simple.

Father, help me to identify my enemies in my life. Help me to see that you are concerned about their lives. Show me how I can pray for them. Show me how I can actively love them. Show me how I can love like Jesus.

September 18

According to the great philosopher Paul McCartney, you "can't buy me love" (that song's been stuck in my head for the last three days). And even though this may be true about love, when you're a single mom of four children, money can still do a whole heck of a lot. And the lack of money can do even more.

You know how when you're young and don't know how the world really works, all of your dreams are huge? "I'll be rich, famous, wildly happy! I'll cure cancer and star in movies and change the world!" we tell ourselves gleefully. Then as we get a little older, the dreams settle down a little. "I'll find my soul mate and get married. We'll have 2.5 children, a dog, and a house with a white picket fence."

we sigh dreamily. Ha. Not that there's anything wrong with dreaming, but life sure doesn't turn out the way we think it will, does it? Fast forward a few years, and we find ourselves as single moms working dead-end jobs just trying to feed the kids and get the bills paid.

I mean, I don't need to be rich. But do I have to be so darn poor? Does it have to be so hard just to live your basic lower-middle-class life, always living paycheck to paycheck, running out of money long before the month's over? And it's not like we're living extravagantly. There are the car payment (and believe me, a single mom absolutely needs a car), the mortgage, grocery bills, clothes for constantly growing kids . . .

I have a friend whose husband makes a lot of money. She doesn't rub it in or anything, but I notice things --that she's wearing a new outfit almost every time I see her, that she's tan and radiant from another spur-of-the-moment vacation, that her nails are perfectly done, that she rarely cooks because her husband takes her to fancy restaurants almost every night. Sigh.

I wish I could say that I'm not jealous, but come on! I don't even need all of that stuff I just listed--just maybe getting to get the kids and me an actual salon haircut instead of cutting our own hair over the bathroom sink. Oh, or how about getting to see movies at the theater instead of waiting for them to show up on TV (which, of course, means severe editing and an abundance of commercials). Or getting to go on an actual vacation to Disney World instead of our normal trip to the local knock-off with its creepy costumes and rickety rides. Even better, paying someone to watch the kids for a week while I went somewhere warm and tropical. Now that would be living.

It's not like I've known any other type of life. I certainly get bombarded with visions of the wealthy life on TV every day, so I'm sure other people don't have to live this way. But me personally? This has been it from day one. My parents weren't rich, and it was a constant source of tension in our house. Then when I took off and disappeared, I had to start all over on my own, attempting to make ends meet with tips earned at a below-average restaurant. Not like I had a ton of expenses then: work, party, eat, party some more, sleep, repeat. Though I must confess that more of my paychecks than I would care to admit went toward supporting some free-loading guys who talked a good game but spent most of their energy on playing video games and listening to rock music. I sure know how to pick them.

But things are starting to look up. I've met someone. Yes, another guy--but this one's different. He's handsome and independent and classy and well, I don't know how else to say it other than he's rich. Really rich. I'm still not sure how it happened. What could a guy like that see in someone like me? Honestly, I'm not looking too hard for that answer, because it sure is nice having someone take me out to dinner and spoil the kids a bit. Okay, so he's a bit bossy, and sometimes he treats me like I'm a child, but still, not worrying about money for once in my life? Almost makes his demeaning comments worth it!

I know that sounds awful, and I know that the guy's money shouldn't matter that much, but it's hard not to think that way when you've been through what I have. What harm is there in just enjoying this situation while I've got it? To be rich just once in my life? Would that be so wrong?

CHAPTER FOUR

Rich People Go Straight to Hell, Do Not Pass Go

The disciples were amazed at his words. But Jesus said again, "Children, how hard it is to enter the kingdom of God! It is easier for a camel to go through the eye of a needle than for a rich man to enter the kingdom of God."
Mark 10:24-25

There are some passages that are easier to dismiss than others. The "eye of a needle" verse in Mark 10:24-25 is one of the easiest of Jesus' wasabi punches to dismiss. When we look at mercy, forgiveness, or even dealing with hate, we all know that we have issues. It's hard for us to dismiss those verses because, if we have any honesty in our bones at all, we know that Jesus has nailed us.

When we read a verse like this, however, and we see the word "rich," we can easily dismiss it as one of the verses that are written for other people. Why is it that we are so dead-set on not being considered rich?

You may remember a guy known as "Joe the Plumber." In early October of 2008 he was just some guy in Toledo, Ohio. By late October, after he went to a political rally right outside of his house and asked then Senator Barack Obama if he was going to raise his taxes, he was riding high on his fifteen minutes of fame.

For the next few weeks, Joe was in the spotlight in a major way. People debated the idea of raising taxes on the "rich" people who made more than a certain amount per year so that those who made less than that could pay less. The craziness that ensued really boiled down to one small question: "am I one of the rich guys or not?"

Actually I am not sure if it was really meant as a question as much as a statement. What Joe was really saying is, "I'm not one of the rich guys! Tax Bill Gates more, but not me!" When we read Jesus' words in Mark we think the same thing: "No way, I am not rich."

We all think we're not rich.

Here is the punch in the gut.

I am rich. You are too.

In fact, you and I are filthy rich. You paid more for this book than most people in the world make in a week. If your income is more than $35,000 per year, you are richer than 95 percent of the people on this planet. I bet that makes you very uncomfortable. If you are like me, you don't feel rich. You feel, at best, middle-class and sometimes, when there seems to be a lot more month than paycheck, you actually feel poor.

There are two basic reasons that we don't think of ourselves as rich.

First is that we just don't *feel* very rich. When we look at our bank accounts, when we see our paychecks, and especially when we see our neighbor's new car, anxiety and envy tell us that we don't have enough.

Second is that when we think of rich people, we think of people who are arrogant, stingy, and wastefully extravagant, and we do not want to be lumped into that group.

But the truth is we are rich. We have what Andy Stanley calls "rich people problems" (*How to Be Rich*, audio CD [North Point Ministries, 2008]).

Here Is One Example: Garage Sales

We have enough money to buy many things that we don't need. So many things that we do not need that we periodically have to set up a bunch of the things we don't need on folding tables that we bought for just such an occasion and wake up at six o'clock in the morning and sell knickknacks for a quarter a piece so we can make a few hundred bucks to buy more stuff that we will eventually sell. Garage sales, now that's a rich person's problem.

Here Is Another: Broken Dishwasher

I pushed the button and no sound came out for a few seconds. I pushed it again, and still nothing. Then water. Lots of water.

Apparently my dishwasher decided to break. Annoying, yes, but no big deal. Until I realized that I would not have a dishwasher for a couple of days. How would the dishes get clean? Would we have to wash them by hand? Where would we put the dirty dishes for a few days if we could not put them in the dishwasher? Dishwashers, now that's a rich person's problem.

I could go on. I don't think that we need to.

Mission Impossible

So if we are all rich (say it with me: "I am rich"), let's read Jesus' words again and see how they pertain to us.

> *Children, how hard it is to enter the kingdom of God! It is easier for a camel to go through the eye of a needle than for a rich man to enter the kingdom of God.*
>
> *Mark 10:24-25*

There have been some ridiculous theological arguments about this verse. They are almost humorous. Like the gate theory— it claims that the "eye of the needle" was a gate in ancient Jerusalem, and it was really hard for a camel to get through this little gate, so hard that he would have to go on his knees to get through, and thus rich people will just have to go to their knees in prayer and submit to God to get through the gate.

Well, that is one way to look at it. It's very likely the wrong way, but it is one way.

I am not sure about you when you read this verse, but it seems to me that Jesus is being pretty clear here in his words, and I am not sure that a fat camel squeezing through a small gate is exactly what he was trying to communicate.

What Jesus was saying is that a rich person entering the Kingdom is like a camel (a very large camel) trying to fit through an eye of a needle (a very small needle like you sew with, not a gate). That is impossible. If you are rich (and you and I are) it is impossible for you to enter the Kingdom. Now that's a wasabi punch to the gut!

Why is it that we rich people have such a hard time getting into the Kingdom?

First, Because We Are Arrogant

The richer we become, the more we think that our intelligence and our rights increase as well. We think that because we are blessed to have been born in a time and a place where we have every opportunity to earn more and get more, we are somehow smarter and more deserving.

A great example is the Lobster Dude.

You may not have seen this same lobster dude, maybe yours is the steak dude or the retail store dude, but you have seen the dude.

I saw the dude one time, and it made me strive not to become the dude. I was eating dinner with some friends at a pretty nice restaurant. It was the forty-dollar-per-person variety. As we were getting our meal, I noted that the couple beside us had the look of people who would eat here a lot and probably did not think it was as "nice" as we did. In other words, I think although I am rich, they were richer. When I am in a restaurant or any public place for that matter, I am very distracted. (I don't officially have adult ADD, but I think that's only because I have never been tested for it.) So I try very hard not to listen in and watch other people, but I definitely have the spiritual gift of eavesdropping. So I listen in a little as the couple discusses that the server is slow and that they are sure that the order will be wrong. About that time the server brought out the filet and lobster that the gentleman had ordered and before the plate could even hit the table he tossed his napkin toward the plate and said, "clearly by the color of the lobster, it is not cooked properly." (Insert your best fake English accent to really be disgusted.) "Take it back and get one cooked properly this time!" He was not concerned with the server. He was not concerned with the cook. He was not concerned about the feelings of his wife. Because he was deserving of more. And just about the time I am ready to call him an arrogant jerk, I become the dude.

Another time, my wife and I were at a restaurant in town, and the server was not meeting my satisfaction quota. I was rambling on and on about it and being quite ridiculous. It was also during the writing of *this very chapter*. My wife leaned over to me and became the great help-meet that she always is and said, "Shawn, chill out." I needed that. I also was quickly reminded by the Holy Spirit that I was writing this chapter and that I was that dude. Not only am I rich, I am often arrogant.

Second, Because We Are Greedy

Jesus taught us a lot about greed and rich people in a parable that he told about creating margin.

He was teaching thousands when a voice in the crowd yelled "tell my brother he has to split his inheritance with me." I find this interesting because it really points out the fact that we are so selfish. Jesus, the son of God, is teaching people and encouraging them and this guy in the audience sees an opportunity to get "what is his." The funny thing is, a quick study of the Jewish inheritance traditions shows us that it was not even "his." His brother was most likely the older brother and, therefore, the rightful owner of the entire inheritance. So basically this guy is asking that Jesus stop what he is doing and come and be the arbiter of a sibling dispute over money.

Don't you love the way Jesus handles this though? He continues to teach. Jesus was on mission.

> Jesus replied, "Man, who appointed me a judge or an arbiter between you?" Then he said to them, "Watch out! Be on your guard against all kinds of greed; a man's life does not consist in the abundance of his possessions."
>
> *Luke 12:14-15*

Here is what I see in that verse. I may be off, but I think Jesus is saying, "Seriously? Do you think that God sent his only son to earth so that two little boys fighting over who gets the most toys can have a wise teacher to help settle the dispute?" Then he turns to the crowd who just heard his smack-down and warns them, "don't be greedy like this—your life will not be measured by who gets the most toys."

> And [then] he told them this parable: "The ground of a certain rich man produced a good crop. He thought to himself, 'What shall I do? I have no place to store my crops.'"
>
> *Luke 12:16-17*

Now that is a rich-person problem. I have so much stuff, what will I do with it? This guy had such a banner year that he literally did not have enough room to store everything. Jesus continues on:

> Then he said, "This is what I'll do. I will tear down my barns and build bigger ones, and there I will store all my grain and my goods."
>
> *Luke 12:18*

He gets a plan. God has given me so much, I have no idea what to do with it all, so I will need to build more storage space. Here is the principle. God gives us margin and we immediately think we deserve to keep all of it. God gave this rich man who produces a good crop lots and lots of margin—a good crop—and he got greedy and came up with a plan to consume the margin rather than a way to share the margin. Let's contextualize that to our situation a little.

I got a raise! We can get that bigger house now.

We saved a little extra, now we can get that third car.

Blessed by an inheritance, a summer cabin would be awesome.

You get the point. Like me you probably live the point.

As I write this book, the world is in one of the roughest economic downturns that we have ever seen. The very difficult truth is that the underlying issues that caused this economic crisis are not financial—they are spiritual. If we really look at it, five of the seven deadly sins are destroying our communities. Gluttony, sloth, envy, and pride, all driven by greed.

This is the statement of a greedy man.

And I'll say to myself, "You have plenty of good things laid up for many years. Take life easy; eat, drink and be merry."

Luke 12:19

Dave Matthews would sample the sentiments of this farmer when he quoted the Old Testament in the 1990's: "Eat, drink, and be merry / For tomorrow we die" ("Tripping Billies," *Crash* [RCA, 1996]).

Bizarro Kingdom

The farmer thinks he's got it made. "I've got enough to last for the rest of my life," he says, which is a great place to be if all there is to life is this life. It seems like a pretty wise plan. But the difference here is that we are talking about entrance into the Kingdom, and the Kingdom is the *Bizarro World* of the earth.

In the popular DC comics, Bizarro World (also known as Htrae) is a fictional planet where everything is counter and opposite of the real world (also known as Earth). I never really read comic books, but I did watch every episode of *Seinfeld*.

According to Wikipedia's discussion of Bizarro World references in pop culture:

> *The concept of "Bizarro World" is a fundamental element in "The Bizarro Jerry", the 137th episode of the American sitcom Seinfeld. In the episode, Elaine makes a new group of friends who represent inverted types of the normal Seinfeld gang. Jerry labels them a bizarro world. These characters are kind, considerate, curious about the world around them, and good citizens. ("Bizarro World," Wikipedia [retrieved March 10, 2009, from http://en.wikipedia.org/wiki/Bizarro_World])*

Eventually, the "Bizarro" friends kick Elaine out and back to her real world. They just cannot have her in the perfect world with her crass and unladylike ways.

The kingdom of God is the Bizarro World of the earth we live in. Rather than gluttony, sloth, envy, and pride, all driven by greed, the Kingdom is marked by contentment, motivation, peace, and humility, all driven by generosity. The Kingdom is a Bizarro World of sorts. It seems to flip the script on most of our thinking. Where we are selfish, Kingdom living is selfless. Where we are unkind, Kingdom living is kind. Where we are depressed, Kingdom living is full of joy. Where we are greedy, Kingdom living is generous.

The Kingdom on earth "as it is in heaven" is a generous world. A Bizarro World. Jesus shows us that God cannot allow greed to enter this Kingdom, as the rich farmer quickly learns.

> God said to him, "You fool! This very night your life will be demanded from you. Then who will get what you have prepared for yourself?" This is how it will be with anyone who stores up things for himself but is not rich toward God.
>
> *Luke 12:20-21*

Fool is a strong word. Jesus chose to use a strong word about greedy people. Now notice that Jesus is not calling him a fool because he is a rich guy; in fact God is the one who blessed him with a banner year. He's a fool because he doesn't know how to *be* rich.

In fact there are several instances in Scripture where God is very clear that we are to enjoy our blessings.

Moreover, when God gives any man wealth and possessions, and enables him to enjoy them, to accept his lot and be happy in his work—this is a gift of God.

Ecclesiastes 5:19

The rich farmer is a fool because he made financial decisions based purely on this life and not on eternity. He is a fool because he thought that the one with the most toys at the end wins and he was just building more and more toy boxes.

That's not how to be rich. That's how to be selfish. Jesus did not die so we could be selfish.

Put Your Hope in God

While teaching the young pastor Timothy, Paul gives some great advice to us rich folk.

Command those who are rich in this present world [remember, that is you and me] not to be arrogant nor to put their hope in wealth, which is so uncertain, but to put their hope in God, who richly provides us with everything for our enjoyment.

1 Timothy 6:17

"Command," Paul says. That is an emphatic instruction. I think that Paul knew from Jesus' tone when he taught about money that this was serious stuff. He knew that if people could whip this selfish gene, they could start to change the world.

"But put their hope in God," now there is a great 401k plan. That is a plan that does not depreciate and is never uncertain. God has laid out the whole plan in front of us and not just shown us a prospectus or best guess, but shown us the guaranteed return:

life. Not just any life but the life that Jesus gives to us, where all our needs are met emotionally, physically, and spiritually. Jesus wants that for us and he is clear that if we are consumed with our riches we cannot come into the Kingdom. It just will not fit.

I don't know about you, but that thought leaves me scared, dumbfounded, and confused. We may ask ourselves who then can get into the Kingdom? The disciples had the same reaction.

> *The disciples were even more amazed, and said to each other, "Who then can be saved?" Jesus looked at them and said, "With man this is impossible, but not with God; all things are possible with God."*
>
> *Mark 10:26-27*

God made a way. He takes the impossible and makes it possible. He takes our selfishness and gives us a new heart, saving us from our desires and wants and giving us new desires and new wants.

I don't think I really get it, though. I am not sure you do either. Because the disciples showed us just a few years later what this looks like in practice, and it looks pretty different from the way we live today.

> *There were no needy persons among them. For from time to time those who owned lands or houses sold them, brought the money from the sales and put it at the apostles' feet, and it was distributed to anyone as he had need.*
>
> *Acts 4:34-35*

When you read this, do you see the church today? This is the real wasabi moment for me. This is what the church looks like when it truly believes that rich people cannot enter the Kingdom like they are and truly relies on the changing grace of Jesus to flip the switch. No needy persons among them. People selling possessions and giving to those who do not have it. Socialism working because it is based not on a political system but on the Lordship of Jesus.

I wish I could say that I live like this, that my church community looks like this. But it just does not. There are glimpses of this Kingdom: Our small group adopting a single mom and her two girls and giving more money than I thought was possible. The establishment of an *Acts 4* fund at my church that has been able to pay rent and buy groceries for those in our church community who have hit a tough spot. I have seen this put into practice in some small measure, but these are only glimpses.

Most of the time, we look like the man who came directly to Jesus and said he wanted to follow him. You may know him as the "Rich Young Ruler." He came running to Jesus, fell on his knees, and asked what he must do to be saved. He explained that he had lived a good life, kept the commandments, and was ready to be all in. I think he was being honest. But Jesus saw straight to his heart and saw that he was indeed being truthful. He had almost all of it together. But he lacked one thing.

> *Jesus looked at him and loved him. "One thing you lack," he said. "Go, sell everything you have and give to the poor, and you will have treasure in heaven. Then come, follow me." At this the man's face fell. He went away sad, because he had great wealth.*
>
> *Mark 10:21-22*

You may notice I often say, "I don't know what this will look like in your life," and I don't know that here either. But you and I both know that we have to do *something* to defeat this sin of greed that Jesus spoke so passionately about.

What Is Your One Thing?

For some of you it may look like a friend of mine who quit his job and sold his house and all of his possessions because he wanted to invest his life in the lives of AIDS orphans in Africa. That was his one thing.

It could be like another friend of mine who is looking for creative ways to give more above and beyond his tithe so he is downsizing his home. He and his wife are in their late twenties and will be giving up on some of the dream of earning equity in this life so they can earn it in the Kingdom. That is his one thing.

For others it could be like another friend, author Anne Jackson, who has realized that she has a huge platform to put social issues in front of people and in 2008 challenged the blogging community to buy shoes for children who could not afford them. Because of her call to action thousands of pairs of shoes were bought. That is Anne's one thing.

What is your one thing? That thing that Jesus tells you to do, and rather than dropping your head and walking away sad, you decide to be rich and act like a rich person should and hold your head up and walk forward.

TAKE A BITE

So what is it for you, that one thing that you need to start being generous with? Do you have extra? Do you have an idea that could produce extra? Maybe you just have access to people who have extra? You can make a huge difference when you walk forward with your head held high. Pray a bold prayer.

God, show me how rich I am. Show me how selfish I am and then show me that one thing that I am holding back financially from you.

November 7

I've been thinking about my kids a lot lately. Well, technically, I've been thinking about myself in relation to the kids——I can't seem to think of anything except as to how it relates to me, lovely self-centered person that I am. Most of the thoughts have had to do with trying to figure out where that line is, the line between the "mom me" and the "real-person me."

Now, I know moms are real people, but sometimes I feel like I've got two distinct personalities competing for my attention all the time. On one side is the woman who wants to be the perfect mother, who loves her kids passionately, who is fiercely protective of them. But on the other side is the girl who is tired and confused and who would just like to have someone take care of her for a little while.

I mean, I want to be a good mom to them, give them the things I never had, protect them from the things I was never protected from, but sometimes I feel like I don't know where to begin or what that even looks like. I'm still trying to figure my own life out, and when you're raising four kids on your own, that doesn't leave a lot of time to do anything other than take care of them. It never stops. Ever. So all the time I'm mom. And honestly? I find myself missing being just Laura. I kind of wish somebody would have warned me about this!

And no, this line of thought isn't coming out of nowhere. The kids and I have moved in with Dave. I know, I know. I've heard the pastor at the church say it's wrong to live with someone without being married, and that it's not good for the kids. The situation is not perfect, but can I be honest? Dave is gorgeous--unnaturally so. And he's good to us--he buys us what we need, and most of the time what we want. And he looks at me like . . . Well, let's just say I feel wanted and loved in a way I haven't in a long time.

I know this sounds selfish and like I'm making excuses. But really, if I'm happy, won't that be better for the kids? "Better for them." What does that even really mean? With

Dave around, they have a house to live in, plenty of food on the table, clothes and toys and all the latest technology. Isn't that enough?

I saw these parenting books in the church bookstore the other day--all with titles talking about "guarding" and "shepherding" your kids. Confusing, right? I read the back of one of them, and it was talking about how the role of a parent is to help your children grow into the people God designed them to be. Yeah, that's great and all, but how can I help them become the people God means them to be when I'm such a mess? When I'm not even really sure that God does have such grand plans for all of us? When Dave looks at me like he can't live without me and suddenly nothing else matters? When I want to be "just Laura" again?

But sometimes at night when I can't sleep, I look in on the girls and wonder what's to stop them from turning out just like I did. And I look at the boys and wonder how in the world they'll turn out like anything other than all the guys that have passed in my life only to pass back out again. Is it enough just to hope they'll turn out all right?

Sometimes I feel love for them so strong that I feel like my chest is going to explode, and I know at that moment that I would give up anything for them. But as soon as that feeling passes, other less noble ones creep on in, and I convince myself that this life will be fine for them. That they'll turn out okay.

And if I'm going to be completely honest, most of the time I don't think about their future at all. I convince myself that being here with Dave (any guy really), doing what I've done, that it was in their best interest. But deep down, I know we're here because I wanted to be here. Because it made me feel safe and loved and it's what suited me at the moment. I worry how it might be affecting the kids, though.

Jason blew up at one of his sisters the other day for no good reason. I know that he's getting close to being a teenager, but this just didn't feel like adolescent moodiness. There was just something about it, the complete rage I saw. And Mandy flinched --distinctly flinched--when Dave brushed up against her in the hallway yesterday. I don't know, I could just be imagining things. I hope I'm just imagining things.

I'm tired. So tired. And I just don't feel strong enough to do what needs to be done. It's not fair. To the kids. To me. They'll turn out okay, won't they?

CHAPTER FIVE

Jesus, Were You the First Mobster?

And if anyone causes one of these little ones who believe in me to sin, it would be better for him to be thrown into the sea with a large millstone tied around his neck.
Mark 9:42

On December 29, 2005, my entire world changed.

I have only had a few of those types of moments in my life. We all have great moments, but there are just some that really stand out. Like the first time I held Connie's hand when we were in eleventh and twelfth grade or when I looked at her and she said, "I do," those stand out as life-changers.

December 29, 2005, does as well.

It was actually as if someone opened up my skull and burned an imprint on my mind. There is a permanent picture there of the first time I saw those eyes. I will never forget the first moment that I looked at my little girl and "became" a dad.

In that moment I started looking at the world through a new filter. I thought of things as a dad, discussed issues as a dad, worried like a dad, prayed like a dad, and laughed and cried like a dad. Some things changed that I never thought would. I now sing Dora the Explorer's theme song more than I do top-forty songs, notice when a new Mickey Mouse Club House is on the DVR (and kinda like it), call Tootsie Roll Pops "poop pops" (we used them as a reward during potty training), and notice the princess dresses in Target and wonder if they have a "king" outfit as well.

One day while cutting the grass I had my MP3 player on and was rockin' and rollin' when suddenly I realized that I was singing the theme song to Dora out loud at the top of my lungs for all the world to hear. It's a catchy tune.

These are all the little things. There are big things too. I hurt more when I hear about a child being neglected, I become enraged when I read about a child being hurt, and I want to throw up when I hear about children being abused.

Having children has really changed my perspective.

I love my children more than my own life. Loving them has also caused me to love all children more. Jesus loved children. It's hard to believe sometimes, but he loved my children even more than I do.

In fact, he loved them so much that he threw down some very serious words at people who might consider leading them astray.

He basically went mobster on them and said that he would cement their feet up to the ankles and throw them off a bridge into the sea as the first base jumpers. That is intense.

I am given to hyperbole. In fact, it seems like I exaggerate a million times a day (case in point). I have never really thought of Jesus as an exaggerator, though.

I just don't see Jesus as the type of guy who comes home and tells his mom that he has fifteen hours of algebra homework and his teacher is making him read two hundred pages of *A Brief History of the Jewish People* all in one night. He was a straight shooter, wouldn't you agree?

Jesus did use hyperbole, but when it comes to this verse, I don't think that Jesus was exaggerating. On the one hand, it seems that we can take Jesus completely literally, and yet if he is saying what it appears he is saying here then we have a striking contradiction to the teachings of Jesus that seem to suggest "they will know us by our love for each other" and other such notable nice things that Jesus had to say.

So it seems that maybe something is being lost in translation.

I guess that we can chalk it up to the Greek.

I took Greek in college, and then again in seminary, but I have to be honest. I have not the slightest idea of what Greek words mean. Sometimes when I am trying to sound smart I will reference Greek words and opine on what those words mean. I might as well reference the lost language of Atlantis, but luckily for all of us, there are a lot of really smart people out there who have studied Greek (and have a lot more combined years of study than my puny little seminary degree) and can give us a much more educated explanation than I could.

I did a little research into this whole idea of throwing people into the sea if they lead children away from Jesus, and well, here is what the Greek *really* means:

Jesus says it would be better to be thrown into the sea than to lead children away from him.

Yes, the Greek is really similar to our translation.

If you look closely, though, what Jesus is saying is *it would be better*. In other words, what Jesus will do to you will make being thrown into the sea like a Sunday picnic in the park.

Now *that* is a wasabi punch.

"The Children in the Room" Litmus Test

My first ministry position out of college was as a children's pastor. You can really tell a lot about a person by how he or she acts toward children. Sometimes when interviewing for a position on the volunteer team we would have the person come and shadow a current volunteer so we could watch how the person interacted with the children.

Jesus often did this as well. He knew he could see straight to a person's character when by how they treated a child. This is what Jesus did to make his point.

When Jesus heard that his disciples were arguing over which of them was the greatest,

Sitting down, Jesus called the Twelve and said . . . "Whoever welcomes one of these little children in my name welcomes me; and whoever welcomes me does not welcome me but the one who sent me."

Mark 9:35-37

A quick glance through Scripture will show you how serious Jesus was about children.

Good thing we totally understand that, and always take care of our children, right? I mean, it was just those mean Romans and the barbarians in the Middle Ages that had children as slaves and such, right? Surely no children are slaves in the world today, right?

Wrong!

According to the International Justice Mission website (http://www.ijm.org/):

Today, millions of lives around the world are in the grip of injustice. More children are held in slavery right now than over the course of the entire trans-Atlantic slave trade. . . . Trafficking in humans generates profits in excess of **12 billion dollars a year** *for those who . . . sell human lives into slavery and sexual bondage.*

More than **2 million children are trapped in forced prostitution.** *. . . And though police should be protectors, in many nations, their presence is a source of insecurity for the poor.*

And just when you are ready to sigh that at least that is in the dark third-world countries, take this big bite of wasabi from my friend Greg Atkinson (www.GregAtkinson.com):

Ignorant, apathetic or active? Which are you? Up until the summer of 2008, I lived as ignorant. I don't mean ignorant in a negative way, as some interpret it. I mean ignorant as it is truly defined: "lacking knowledge or information as to a particular subject or fact . . . uninformed; unaware."

Until recently in my life, I thought that slavery was something of the past. I thought we, as a country, had moved on since Lincoln and the Civil War, etc. and were truly the "land of the free" as our national anthem suggests. I had heard of overseas sex slaves like in Thailand or Cambodia, or even Russia, but I thought these were rare and not really a serious problem.

Here was my wake-up call: I was speaking to church leaders in Atlanta and I asked them what they were burdened about as a city, what they were battling together as the Church (capital "C"). Their answer was "child sex trafficking". My response was "Oh, you mean helping overseas?" They said, "No, right here. Atlanta is number one in the United States for child sex trafficking." My jaw dropped. I was speechless. They went on to tell me of girls as young as five and six years old (my kids' age) that were being sold as sex slaves—in Atlanta!

As a dad with three children, two of them being girls, I started to tear up and felt a pain in my heart and sickness in my spirit that I can't fully describe. They went on to tell me about Las Vegas and Phoenix. The list goes on and on, now that I've been studying and researching it for myself. Just about every major city, including my own city of Dallas, Texas, has human trafficking going on.

Did you know that the twenty-seven million slaves in the world today represent the largest amount of slaves at any one time in history? Plainly put: slavery has never been more prominent than at this time in world history. Slavery is not legal anywhere, but happens everywhere. At least 14,500 slaves are trafficked into the United States each year. Ninety dollars is the average cost of a human slave around the world.

What does that mean? Friend, that means that you have now left the "ignorant" category. You, reading this, now have to choose between apathy and action.

I refuse to be apathetic to something I believe is so close to God's heart. See, I'm a parent and I can't stand when my child scrapes their knee. If I see tears in my child's eyes it breaks my heart. When I think of the children all around the world that are forced to do unthinkable things and cry out (literally) night after night for someone to rescue them

. . . I can not fathom what our Heavenly Father must feel as he hears his precious children around the world calling out for help.

This should shake us up. This should make us angry. It made Jesus use fightin' words, and yet it seems to me that as Christians we are not as serious about this as Jesus was. What should this make us do? Maybe if we find out how Jesus treated children that would help.

So what was it that Jesus saw in children that made him use such harsh words against those who would harm them? Hint: it's not just that they are cute.

Jesus Said We Should Be More Like Children

And he said: "I tell you the truth, unless you change and become like little children, you will never enter the kingdom of heaven. Therefore, whoever humbles himself like this child is the greatest in the kingdom of heaven.
Matthew 18:3-4

All of us know that there are challenges with children, but my experience has been that most of the time when I am frustrated with my children, it is because I have allowed a negative behavior or habit to form in them. In other words, yes, it is your parents' fault.

The truth is I have learned more from my little girl than I will ever teach her about how I should live and the way that I should love God. The way she loves me and her mom and the way she lives her life is really a model of what life could be like in many ways. Jesus saw this. That is why he said that we should come to him like a child.

There are a few characteristics of children that Jesus saw that are worthy of our aspirations:

Joy

My daughter's laughter is contagious around our house. It brings smiles to our faces and it makes us laugh. All I have to do is bring some tickle-bugs out or make the noise that a humpback whale makes (or at least the sound I imagine they would make) and her joy comes out. I love her joy because it is not contrived. She has a joy in life that experiences and failures too often strip from us as we age. She does not take herself too seriously and is willing to laugh at herself. In fact, she takes after her daddy and will do just about anything to make you laugh. Jesus loved that about children. You know that he laughed with them. He played games with them. He tickled them until they could not breathe and then gave them a second to gulp in air and tickled some more. Jesus wants us to have that joy as well.

Innocence

In his typical, countercultural way, Jesus loved the innocence of children. Judaism didn't emphasize a child's innocence, but rather a child's immaturity and foolishness. The religious leaders would have scoffed at this notion that we should act like a child as a ridiculous statement, rather having children be seen and not heard. Jesus saw an innocence in this "immaturity" that was to be sought after. Would you not agree that we have lost our innocence in many ways? We call it "maturing" the first time a teenager drops a curse word, or the first time a fourteen-year-old girl has sex, we call it an "experience." We have been desensitized and spiritually neutered to the point that nothing surprises us. Nothing deplores us. Nothing breaks our hearts. A child's heart is easily broken.

When my daughter was just a few weeks shy of two years old I got the bright idea that we should watch *Rudolf the Red-nosed Reindeer*. We were not five minutes in before she was in tears at how the other reindeer (especially his dad, who is a real jerk) were treating Rudolf. I know it's juvenile, but maybe we have lost the ability to care if Rudolf is mistreated. Work with me here. There are Rudolfs in our world that children care about and we should too. Jesus saw that.

Openness and Trust

Children come running to Jesus with complete openness and trust. They have no fear of him and know that he has their best interest at heart. This is a characteristic that I long for in my relationship to Jesus. Complete openness with him. Complete trust. My daughter trusts me completely. There is nothing that she will not share with me. There is nothing that she will not ask me to wipe off of her. Snotty nose, messy butt, skinned knee—she trusts her dad to take care of it. I think that Jesus saw that in the little children. They were open with him. They were not trying to hide their sins—there were no pretenses—they were just real. Jesus loved that.

Jesus Didn't Just Talk About Children— He Engaged Them

When Jesus saw this, he was indignant. He said to them, "Let the little children come to me, and do not hinder them, for the kingdom of God belongs to such as these. I tell you the truth, anyone who will not receive the kingdom of God like a little child will never enter it." And he took the children in his arms, put his hands on them and blessed them.

Mark 10:14-16

The disciples had mission drift. They were caught up in the moment and were dismissing the children around Jesus and not letting them get close to him. It's easy to be critical of the disciples here but there have been times in all of our lives where we were so concerned about "church" or "ministry" or even our family vacation that we lose sight of the fact that it is all about people. We can get so caught up in the plan that we forget the plan was for the people involved. Many trips to the mall around Christmas have produced such forgetfulness.

So Jesus gets ticked off at the disciples (righteously ticked off, mind you) and tells them to let the children come to him. Jesus did not just talk about children; he really loved them and wanted to be around them. He engaged them. He talked to them. He held them. He loved them.

David was that kind of man. At our church he was known by most of the children as "the lollipop man." More important to me, my little girl loved him. David would sit right outside of my daughter's class at church with a basket of lollipops and give each child one (sometimes two if they were real sweet) to make their church experience even better. As soon as I picked Isabelle up from her class, the first thing she would say was not, "hey, dad," or "I had fun," or even "I learned so much." She just always asked, "Can we see the lollipop man?" The unique thing about David was that in my many years at Seacoast, David said very few words to me. He was a painfully shy man and never did very well around adults. But when he saw a child happy because he had given them a lollipop, his eyes grew brighter and a smile would come across his face. It's funny—I know that there is not a ton of "spiritual" stuff going on here but I think this love of children and just engaging them made Jesus smile too. Handing out lollipops to the several hundred children every weekend was his small way of being like Jesus.

When I found out that the lollipop man had cancer, my heart hurt. I knew my daughter would not remember him, and I wished I had gotten a picture of them together. There are thousands of parents who wait to see Jesus' face when he smiles at the lollipop man. David never preached a sermon and may not be remembered by many. But he preached a sermon with his life, and I will remember him forever.

Jesus Said That the Way You Treat a Child Is the Way You Treat Him

Whoever welcomes one of these little children in my name welcomes me; and whoever welcomes me does not welcome me but the one who sent me.

Mark 9:37

Jesus equated the way we treat children with the way we treat him and his father. I mean, think of this scenario. What if someone were to come up to me while I am holding my little boy and say, "Man, I really enjoyed your book and your teaching and preaching have touched my life. Thank you"? That would be cool, but what if as they were walking away they said, "oh, and one more thing" and just hauled off and slapped my little boy in the face?

I am not a violent person. But there would commence a smackdown on somebody like there had never been before. I really don't care how much you like me if you hurt my children. No amount of good words, money, time, gifts, or anything in the world can make up for that. I think that is how Jesus feels when we mistreat children. If we worship him and yet we are unkind to children, if we pray to him and yet will not give children the time of day, if we serve in his name yet will not serve a child in need, then let the smack-down commence.

One of the great things about children is their innocence. There is nothing like knowing that although sinful at their nature, children are so full of innocence. People who hurt children are robbing them of this innocence that is so wonderful.

A young man wanted to talk to me one time and said that he had something that he had to get off of his chest. As we talked about some of the anger issues he was dealing with, he confessed some of the self-esteem and even self-hate that he was projecting into his relationships with others, and finally the dam broke and he was just overtaken by tears and grief. He then said that he needed to tell me something that he had never told anyone. When he was seven years old an uncle had started to show him pornography. That escalated into physical sexual abuse eventually even involving other children as well. This abuse had so confused this little boy that now as a twenty-year-old he was afraid that he himself would do the same to other children. He was struggling with his desires while trying to carry on with "life as normal" on the outside.

Over the next few years I would walk through this situation with this young man seeing him tell his parents, sitting in on counseling sessions, and even watching at one point as he torpedoed out of control into a depression and almost died of an eating disorder. It makes me weep even now to think that this whole situation started for a seven-year-old. When he should have been watching *Transformers* or *G.I. Joe*, some pervert had him watching pornography. When he should have been daydreaming about his first kiss, he had already had sexual atrocities carried out on him that we would shudder to think about. His innocence was stolen. He had been forced to lie and had to deal with this for thirteen years all by himself.

You can see why Jesus was so intense when he spoke of people who hurt children. When we hurt a child, we are literally hurting Jesus. In his description of the last judgment, Jesus emphasized that the way we treat "the least of these" is the way we treat him. Will we hear and answer their cry—Jesus' cry? As Christ-followers we are to be a people who protect the innocence of children and the lives of children. This should be a part of our DNA, as it was Jesus'.

TAKE A BITE

I am not sure how I sleep knowing that there are children (some the same age as my children) in the world who are being abused, molested, and sold into slavery right now. Somehow my mind shuts down and allows me to sleep. But I need less sleep. I need to care more about their situation. I need to feel the gut-wrenching punch that reminds me that if I do nothing, I am making a choice to allow these atrocities to continue. Let me echo the words of the Jewish philosopher Hillel, who said:

"If not me, who? If not now, when?"

Will you join me in swallowing this extra-painful glob of wasabi?

God, help me change the world by investing in the lives of children—children in my family, children in my community, and children in my world. God show me how my "maturity" has stolen my innocence and return to me the heart of a child. In doing this, Jesus, let me know you better and trust you more.

January 13

I think I've finally worked up the courage to leave Dave—to pack up the kids and our stuff (minus some rather nice clothes and toys that were provided by the man himself—seems a bit rude to take them with us, doesn't it?), to get out of this situation that more and more appears to be just wrong, and to start over somewhere else. None of the kids have actually admitted that he has hurt them in any way, but I see the look in their eyes when he's around. I should know that look. I saw it in the mirror every day when I was young. And as much as I'm enjoying the perks of living with a man who may not treat me like a queen but at least doesn't expect me to pay the bills, I just can't stomach the thought that my kids might turn out like me because I was too weak to protect them.

Wow, that sure sounds strong and confident and self-sacrificing, doesn't it? Truth be told, I haven't started packing yet. And I haven't really mentioned it to anybody --Dave or the kids. And I've only just begun entertaining the thought of looking for a new place to go. It's just that this is a strange situation for me to be in. In the past, I had already found the next guy before I had left the old one --I'm not one to leap without making sure there's a net that I've already tested, if you know what I mean. This time, it's not like I have a job or family or a relationship to go to. It seems a lot safer, and even smarter, to just stay here where I know we'll have a roof over out heads and food on the table, but somehow I just know I have to leave this place.

I don't know if it's the church I've been going to, or if it might be the parenting book that I'm reading (yep, I sucked it up, went back to the church bookstore, and bought that parenting book), or if it's just something in the air, but I'm finally starting to think maybe, just maybe, there's something better out there for me and for the kids. There's this Bible verse that the pastor read at church last week that says something about God knowing the plans he has for us, and that these plans are for good. I just--well, I don't know--I think I'm starting to hope that that's true. I really want to believe it, that our lives aren't just going to be a cycle of bad relationship after bad relationship. This can't be all there is, can it?

But here's what makes me nervous--if God does have plans for us, that could mean anything! It could mean he's going to send us to the jungle in the middle of nowhere to live in grass huts while we try to tell people about Jesus when we don't even speak the same language. It could mean that someday I'm going to end up going door to door in an ugly outfit with no make-up on handing out pamphlets and telling people they're going to hell. Or (I shudder to think) it could mean that I'm going to have to be celibate the rest of my life!

I kind of get the feeling that if I choose that route --choose to follow Jesus--that I won't be able to do it halfway. I think that maybe if I do that, then I have to turn my back on everything I know. That's a scary thought, isn't it? Because honestly, I want to know Jesus and to be in a relationship with him, but I also want to keep doing what I've always done. There's a reason I haven't changed very much over the years--it's much easier to keep living the way I've been living than to face something new or unknown. In other words, I'm lazy!

Some of those TV preachers make it seem like God's just out there wanting to make me happy and to give me stuff. But then the pastor at my church started talking about sacrifice and persecution and discipline and facing difficulties, all for following Jesus. Sure, if I was certain that I loved him. But I'm not even sure if I believe in him.

All I know is that I'm restless and ready for a change. All I know is that I want things to be different, that I want to be different. But deep down, I'm afraid being different will be hard, that it will hurt and take work. And most of all, I'm afraid I won't be able to handle it and that I'll just go back to my old life. And this is when those thoughts start creeping in: Is it worth the pain? Is your current life really that bad? If there is a God, why would God care about what you do with your life anyways?

How many times have I tried to change and failed? What makes me think that this time will be any different? I don't know; maybe it won't be. But maybe, just maybe, there's something better out there waiting.

CHAPTER SIX

What If I Use a Rearview Mirror?

*Jesus replied, "No one who puts his hand
to the plow and looks back is fit
for service in the kingdom of God."*
Luke 9:62

Have you ever wondered what Jesus meant by "fit for service in the kingdom"? When you first read this verse it is easy to think of it simply as a warning against a crooked life. You know, do the right things, keep your path straight, "don't cuss, don't chew, and don't dance with girls who do." But the core of Jesus' statement here is so much wider than some works-based religion. The statement is quite revealing about what Jesus sees as one of the few things that would make a Christ-follower unfit for serving in his Kingdom. We know from the Old Testament that to God, looking back is a big deal—think pillar of salt (Genesis 19:24-26)—and now we see the phrase *like father like son* applies in this situation as well.

This is one of the ample examples of Jesus' teachings that go well beyond salvation and into painting a picture of what someone who serves in his Kingdom would look like. Jesus teaches on this subject by doing what he did so well, using a modern-day illustration to show truth. The problem for us is that modern to Jesus was A.D. 32 or so. Most of us reading this book do not live in an agrarian society. Sometimes this makes some of the illustrations in the Bible hard to understand. When Jesus starts talking about farmers building bigger barns, seeds falling on the side of the road, or yokes being easy, he might as well be using space travel illustrations because I have been to the moon exactly the same number of times as I have plowed a field. Because of this, we have to dig a little deeper into some of the statements of Jesus to try and see exactly what he was teaching.

Speaking of digging deep (did you like how I did that?), Jesus uses the illustration of a plow in Luke chapter 9. Apparently Jesus is pretty serious about plowing in a straight line because in verse 62 he gets pretty miffed at the idea of someone looking back while plowing. Just a casual reading of this verse would have us thinking that Jesus was taking his farming a little too seriously.

Maybe we would understand this better with a modern—for us—illustration.

You probably have mowed a lawn before or at least hired someone else to mow it for you, right? When I was about ten years old, I took over the lawn-mowing duties of our family and several decades later I am still mowing lawns. I think I will start my son early. As I said earlier, I may have never been officially diagnosed with ADD, but I have always had a touch of EDD (easily distracted disorder) if nothing else. You can ask my wife. I remember many times mowing the lawn and being distracted by friends riding by on their bikes, the next-door neighbor's dog barking, or just a daydream, and the next thing you know I would be mowing in a crooked line. If you push the lawn mower while looking back over your shoulder, you'll be mowing a crooked line very quickly. That's not so bad, because you can correct it by mowing over your mistake. But if you are plowing, you've made a crooked line and that means that you have to keep making crooked lines to match. I am not the sharpest blade on the plow, but the best I can imagine, that would mean that you would have made a total disaster of the field.

Jesus knew this.

First, because he lived in a society where he saw fields all the time.

Second, because he was God and knows everything. Sometimes that just seems unfair.

Jesus knew that looking back could also mess up our lives.

First, because he saw people do it all the time.

Second, because he is God and knows everything. Again, unfair but true.

The Bible has a lot of stories about great people doing unbelievable things for God. It seems that even these great people had a touch of EDD. A thorough reading of the Bible finds it difficult to find Bible characters who at some point were not distracted by their lives prior to meeting Christ or some life they never got to live.

Adam and Eve were distracted by an apple (looks like Steve Jobs was already at work). Then there was Lot's wife and that whole pillar of salt thing again.

Noah.

Abraham.

Sarah.

Isaac.

Jacob.

Moses.

Elijah.

Jonah.

And pretty much every other character we encounter were all guilty of mowing the lawn a little crooked. Even Peter, Jesus' friend and member of his inner circle, got distracted right in front of Jesus, sinking in the water. At least we are not alone in getting distracted.

But the deal is, I want not just to enter the Kingdom and get my ticket to go to heaven, I want to serve in the Kingdom that we see glimpses of here on earth.

Jesus has a little wasabi punch to the gut for many of us when he tells us why that may be easier said than done.

Here is the story in context.

> As they were walking along the road, a man said to him, "I will follow you wherever you go."
> Jesus replied, "Foxes have holes and birds of the air have nests, but the Son of Man has no place to lay his head."
> He said to another man, "Follow me."
> But the man replied, "Lord, first let me go and bury my father."
> Jesus said to him, "Let the dead bury their own dead, but you go and proclaim the kingdom of God."
> Still another said, "I will follow you, Lord; but first let me go back and say good-by to my family."
> Jesus replied, "No one who puts his hand to the plow and looks back is fit for service in the kingdom of God."
>
> *Luke 9:57-62*

It's great to study Bible passages in their context. It helps us understand the whole picture. But some people who dissect the Bible like it is a frog lying on their seventh grade science lab table can find some weird teachings in the Bible. I have learned that you can make an argument for just about anything if you can take the right verse out of context. That is the case with this passage as well. Some have really tried to narrow this passage down a lot. In some ways they have stripped the passage of so much of its meaning that it smells a little like that frog—dead, stale, and only useful for staring and gawking at.

In some circles the teaching on this passage has been narrowed down to one statement: being distracted by your family is sin.

That is just silly. And it makes Jesus look a little silly.

Work with me here. If it really boiled down to just a man wanting to bury his *dead* father, shouldn't he bury his father? I think Jesus would have hugged him, mourned with him, and gone to the funeral with him.

If it is only about saying goodbye to loved ones, shouldn't we be kind and respectful to our families and spend quality time with them before leaving home for an indefinite period of time?

As a son, I live seven houses down from my parents and about seventeen houses down from my mother-in-law so that I can take care of them.

As a husband, I put time with my wife as the highest priority on my schedule. I make sure we have a date night each week, quality time together each night, and a few moments of connection during each workday.

As a father, I spend not just quality time but quantity time with my children and think that being a dad to them is of highest importance.

I know that you do these things too.

So am I wrong? Are you wrong?

So What Did You Really Mean, Jesus?

Now, it would be a *really* shocking wasabi moment (and would probably sell a few more books) if I were to suggest you should actually disown your family. Some have actually done this and have offered a side of Kool-Aid. I am not so sure some of you would be ready to drink that Kool-Aid, and I am pretty sure that was not what Jesus was pointing us to.

Jesus is giving us the truth about ourselves. He is pointing out how easily we are distracted by stuff—especially the stuff in our lives that we left behind for Jesus—and if we look back we are not fit for the Kingdom. At first blush, that may seem a little benign in comparison to slapping your mother-in-law and giving your dad the cold shoulder, but the truth is, it's an even bigger deal (and slapping your mother-in-law is a pretty big deal).

What Jesus is teaching is that if we look back, take a second glance if you will, at the mistress that is our former life (or even a life we never had)—we are not fit to serve in the Kingdom. We have essentially turned into a spiritual pillar of salt, useless to do anything that God has created us to do.

Jesus mentions Lot's wife again in Luke.

> Likewise, no one in the field should go back for anything. Remember Lot's wife! Whoever tries to keep his life will lose it, and whoever loses his life will preserve it.
>
> Luke 17:31-33

This is a big deal.

God saved us and changed our whole beings so that we could serve in the Kingdom. Many people will translate this into a statement regarding salvation, but I am not sure that is where Jesus was going. He didn't say, "If you look back you will not go to heaven." Sometimes we get so caught up in heaven that we become, as they say, "so heavenly minded we're of no earthly good." As a pastor, often I have been encouraging someone to step it up in their lives and really go to another level for Jesus and they say, "Are you saying that I am going to hell?" Your counsel then goes straight to hell, doesn't it? As long as we can stay out of hell, we think that it is all good. The truth is, however, that there is so much more to the Kingdom and God's purpose for our lives than just getting into heaven. So much, it will blow your mind.

This world is a great example of people who desperately want to press forward and be about the future only to be distracted by the past and stall out. So how do we avoid this wayward, crooked line in our lives? What can we learn through the wasabi punch to the gut Jesus had for these young men in this scripture?

Distraction Can Destroy

I remember playing little league football. I played for the Moncks Corner Cowboys and was a receiver and back-up quarterback. I have always had a pretty good memory, so my job was to run every other play. I was one of the younger boys on the team and as a sixth grader weighed in at just slightly larger than a third-grade girl. I ran in plays that rarely (well, let's be honest, never) included getting the ball thrown to me. Until one game when, for some reason, the coach decided to have me run a play that actually included me. I was pumped. It was the big play. I would catch the ball, then I would run and make a move on some other little boy and leave him standing in awe as I ran past him for a touchdown. The coach would see the error of his ways and my number would be called a whole lot more. All this went through my little brain as I ran in the play. Then I took off down the field, surprisingly fast for a third-grade girl, and ran my route perfectly. The ball came sailing toward me, and I looked up to see whom I would be faking out and leaving in the dust when I felt the ball hit my shoulder pad and bounce to the ground. I was distracted. I had taken my eye off the ball. I had lost sight of the goal and looked ahead to the field. Poop.

I never was thrown the ball again in my illustrious four-month-long football career. In my opinion, "the catch" (or lack thereof) is to blame for the absence of my professional football career. It knocked me down about 400,000 draft slots in the NFL. Who knows what could have been?

My football career is really no big deal. I have gotten over it. But my life and your life is a huge deal. It is an especially big deal to Jesus. He died for our lives.

Imagine a terrible fire in a building, and you are trapped in that building. You have no idea how to get out; in fact, you don't even know the extent of the fire because you are so lost in the building. So suddenly a fireman comes in and calls to you that you need to leave. You are hesitant at first because you don't realize that the fire is as bad as it is. Finally, you are so overtaken by the smoke that you collapse in his arms, and he drags you out of the fire to your safety. After a few groggy moments you stand up and start to walk away with the fireman and have the strangest desire. The desire to look back. The desire to go back.

Absurd, isn't it? Who would desire such a thing?

Jesus saved us and as soon as we can get our bearing, it seems as if we begin to look over our shoulder glancing fondly at the fire that nearly burned us to our death. That is a whacked-out desire. Our desires are evil, and we need new ones. The only way to do that is by submitting our will to God's will and making his desires our desires.

Wanting What God Wants

As the psalmist says:

Delight yourself in the LORD
and he will give you the desires of your heart.

Psalm 37:4

Many have taken this verse and perverted it to mean that if we will just serve God, he will give us every little thing we want. In other words, if you start serving God and one of your desires is a Hummer, if you will just "name it and claim it," a Hummer is yours. Marriage is a great example of how untrue this is. Any couple worth their salt knows that each one has to lay down his or her desires and submit to the other's in order to really make a relationship work. Most of the struggling couples I see have challenges coming from one of the two deciding that all of the desires that they brought into the relationship should be fulfilled. That is selfishness. That is not delighting in your spouse.

Delighting in God means it is God's desires that matter, not yours. Just like Peter's desires as he walked the streets just after Jesus' crucifixion, our desires often deny the truth and hold onto the past, but old sins and old attachments are totally inferior to the great things God wants for us. Our desires tap us on the shoulder and have us looking back rather than walking forward.

The great thing is, though, that if we will delight in God, it will change our desires, thus making our desires his desires, and then he can give us what *we* want because it is what *he* wants. Kinda sounds like God is a control freak, doesn't it. He is. With good reason. He is God.

I am not God, but sometimes I get to play one as dad. My daughter loves to pretend to drive our car while we are unloading the groceries. The car is always safely parked in the garage and she cannot reach the pedals, so we are pretty safe. One day, however, she got a little wise in her own eyes and decided that she wanted to "real" drive the car and not just "tend" drive the car (that would be "pretend" for those of you who don't speak three-year-old). That was her desire. In her little mind, she thought she could handle it.

As a dad, I am a control freak and would not let her drive the car at three years old. Good time to be a control freak, don't you think?

That is what happens when we let ourselves be deceived into thinking that our desires are good. James gives us a little insight into what our desires look like.

> But each one is tempted when, by his own evil desire, he is dragged away and enticed. Then, after desire has conceived, it gives birth to sin; and sin, when it is full-grown, gives birth to death.
>
> James 1:14-15

We are evil. That seems to be a consistent theme in the Bible. We need to come to a place where we realize that we are the ones who invent the hideous plans in our minds, conjure the situations of sin, and devise plans to destroy. The devil does not make us do it, God does not tempt us, and it is not a test. It is in our very nature.

If You Give a Mouse a Cookie

My daughter has a book that she loves by Laura Numeoff, called *If You Give a Mouse a Cookie*. The book is the silly account of the craziness that can occur once you give a mouse a cookie. Then he will want milk, then he will spill the milk, then he will have to take a bath, and on and on until finally he is so worn out that he will ask for another cookie. The same is true with our desires. If you give your desires a nibble, they will want more and the next thing you know, they (as James says) *entice us and drag us away.*

We think we can handle our lives. We cannot. James paints a great picture here of how it will go down if we try. We will look back and when we do, the look will turn into a stare, then into sin. Our desires will hold us back, dragging us away from the life that Jesus has planned for us, and they will drag us away into a place where we get carried away and think that we know what is best for our lives. We don't. God does.

Here is the deal with you and me. We want to drive our own lives. We can't reach the pedals and we are totally clueless, but we think we can do it. Am I wrong? God says, "Not on my watch, buddy. I am a control freak." Because God knows that the final destination of that wayward drive is death.

But if we will delight ourselves in him, then he will drive, and we will see for ourselves that he is all we will ever need. Psalm 1 puts it like this,

> *Blessed is the man*
>   *who does not walk in the counsel of the wicked*
>   *or stand in the way of sinners*
>   *or sit in the seat of mockers.*
> *But his* **delight** *is in the law of the LORD,*
>   *and on his law he meditates day and night.*
> *He is like a tree planted by streams of water,*

which yields its fruit in season
and whose leaf does not wither.
Whatever he does prospers.

Psalm 1:1-3 (emphasis added)

If we stay close to God's desires, we will avoid sin.

It is that simple. Not easy. But pretty simple.

The psalmist continues in Psalm 1:4 and paints a little different picture for those who are distracted by sin.

Not so the wicked!
They are like chaff
that the wind blows away.

Psalm 1:4

Do ou ever struggle to figure out what delighting in God looks like? My carnal nature makes me think of sitting aimlessly and smiling at flowers. You may have a different scene in mind. But I think that Jesus gives us a better picture.

If not delighting in God means we look back at all the things God asked us to abandon, and looking back makes us unfit for service in the Kingdom, a little theological math would say that delighting in God would look a whole lot like serving in the Kingdom. Richard Baxter, a seventeenth-century Puritan minister, hoped that "delighting in [God] may be the work of our lives" (*The Saints' Everlasting Rest* [Grand Rapids, Mich.: Baker Book House, 1978], 17).

So how do we delight?

We serve with our eyes straight ahead. We make every day about others. We take the attitude of Christ. We don't look back with a wayward eye but instead with steady focus we keep pressing forward.

Don't look back. There is nothing in the burning building worth saving.

TAKE A BITE

What causes you to look back? I could list a hundred things, but the truth is you know eactly what it is. Why don't you call it what it is? Distraction and desires that will lead to sin. Find someone who can pray with you and ask you difficult questions in your life.

Father, I am so drawn to look over my shoulder at what was and what could have been. I want my desires to be your desires as I delight in you. I am asking you to change my desires and make me more like you.

February 10

It took a few weeks, but I finally managed to leave Dave and to get my kids and me out of this situation! I know deep down it's a good thing, but a thought struck me the other day --you know, one of those thoughts that was probably there all along but you've buried in the corner of your brain and chosen to ignore? It came when I was shuffling through all the questions of what life will be like now. Will all our problems be suddenly magically solved? Will I do anything differently next time? Will the kids be less angry and resentful? Will things really be any better?

And that's when the thought came like a mental slap to the face. All these years, I've been counting on other things to fix my life: making more money, moving to a new city, finding a man, leaving a man, getting better friends, getting a better job. Or even counting on being able to change myself: being nicer, trying harder, swearing less. I've tried and tried to find the thing that will just make my life better. I've tried and tried to find the thing that will make me different. And none of this trying has made the slightest bit of difference. Stings, doesn't it?

It's kind of like me and clothes. I can put on a nice outfit, high-heeled shoes, do my hair, and put on all kinds of makeup—trust me, when I make this type of effort, I look pretty good. I look like I have it all together, that I have a good life and I'm something to see. But in reality, I'll be completely uncomfortable all day long, and at the first opportunity I'll head for home, put on sweats and a ratty T-shirt, wipe off the makeup, and pull my hair into a ponytail. I can work at looking good on the outside, but it doesn't change that I'm a ratty T-shirt type of girl, and I always will be. That's why I've never wanted to go on one of those makeover shows, because I know they would spend all the time and money making me look good, and I'd be back to my normal self within the month.

So if making all these changes isn't working, what do I do instead? If working this hard at fixing myself and my life hasn't actually changed anything, then what? Do I <u>stop</u>

working at it? What good would that do? Ugh, this is just too confusing. And exhausting. I think I deserve a trip to Starbucks to help me think through this, no?

In all seriousness, it does seem that the problems in my life are a lot deeper than where I live or whom I spend time with. They come out of who I am at my very core. It's time to make a major change--not just in my address, but in my heart.

At church this weekend, they read this verse about things flowing from our hearts, that good things come from good hearts, and evil things come from evil hearts. I never thought of myself as evil--that seems pretty extreme, almost like a comic book bad guy, Lex Luthor or the Joker plotting to take over the world (can you tell I have sons?). But I certainly haven't found myself surrounded by much good stuff either. So does this mean that my bad decisions and rough life are the result of sin? That I am, in fact, evil?

That sounds pretty scary--especially since I don't want to be evil or try to be evil--but I really think it may be true. I need a new heart. I need a good heart. I need my old self ripped right out and a new one put in. Am I ready to let God do that, though? I had this picture Bible when I was a kid, and I remember some guy wrestling with God. They were both pretty buff in the picture, but I am pretty sure God won. I bet he will win with me too. Maybe it's time I consider a surrender. Even saying that is hard for me to swallow. It hurts for me to admit that I have been wrong all this time, and I bet it will hurt to let go of my old heart.

But it almost sounds worth it. Am I ready for it?

So—Jesus, What Happens When I Don't Have Any Limbs Left to Cut Off?

And if your right hand causes you to sin, cut it off and throw it away. It is better for you to lose one part of your body than for your whole body to go into hell.
Matthew 5:30

Traveling back from a speaking engagement about four hours from my home, I decided to call just after lunchtime and check in on my wife and my daughter, who was then two and a half years old. I knew they would probably be outside playing, but I wanted to tell my little girl that I loved her and missed her before she went down for a nap.

After a few more rings than normal, my wife answered the phone. It was one of those answers that

CHAPTER SEVEN

sounded like she was wrestling a mule with one arm while she was trying to answer the phone with the other. As she started I could tell that I had called at an "inopportune parenting moment." It seemed as if the child had decided to die and was willing to take mommy with her. It was not good. "Shawn, just a moment . . . no, don't touch it . . . Shawn, just a . . . mommy said 'no' . . ."

Then I started to hear, in the smallest little voice in the background, my daughter's side of this drama that was unfolding. "But I want to touch the poop, mommy! I want to touch the poop!"

Yes, you read that right, and I heard it right. My beautiful (and quite girly) little girl was pleading to touch the poop. My wife then suggested that I call back in a few minutes. I willingly agreed, realizing that I had, well, stepped into the middle of the poop.

When I called back about a half hour later, I got the full story. (After thirty minutes of wondering "whose poop?" I really needed the full story.)

Apparently, because I was gone the night before, I had not been there to clean up the latest dog poop left by our miniature dachshund. (My absence, more specifically my not picking up the poop, had caused a greater disruption than I would have imagined.) Playing in our backyard is not a new activity, and is in no way out of the normal schedule. But for some reason on this day, our daughter was drawn to the poop. She wanted—nay, needed—to touch the poop. The discussion that I unwittingly stumbled upon was my wife trying to convince her to not touch the dog's poop.

She was on the way to some great playtime on her play set, but got distracted along the way and became determined to touch the poop.

Now why would someone want to touch the poop? Surely we can just chalk this one up to the strange desires of a two-year-old right? I mean, come on, as adults we never want to do something like that.

Do you ever want to touch the poop? God has some unbelievable things planned for you, but like a two-year-old who has a fabulous play set, you get upset and stomp your feet because you would rather touch the poop.

Most of you (well, let's even go out on a limb and say all of you) would say "no," but first let me briefly define "the poop."

What if we were to define poop as something gross and disgusting in our life?

What if we were to define gross and disgusting as anything outside the will of God?

What if we were to define anything outside the will of God as sin?

Now. Let me ask that question again. Do you ever want to touch the poop?

I do.

I think you probably do as well.

Is there a sin in your life that eats your lunch?

You have tried to shake it, but the truth is you are being destroyed by it.

This world, in fact, is full of great examples of people who desperately want to touch the things in our lives that God has called off limits.

The man who is reading this book right now but will surf the web for pornography before the day is over? Poop.

The woman who continues an inappropriate relationship online with an old high school flame even though she knows it's destructive to her marriage? Poop.

The young engaged couple who has vowed to stop having sex until the wedding, but nonetheless makes plans to be alone tonight so that they can intentionally sin and then call it a mistake again? Poop.

The author who has written the last eighty-three words with ease but has his own poop to deal with as well? Poop happens.

Avoid Stepping in It

We know these sins are nothing but poop. But the problem is most of it seems to attack us from within our minds. This is the scary sin that is not easily discarded and in our hearts we think may actually beat us in the end.

What does Jesus have to say about the scary sin? You know, the sin that is scary like a clown, only sometimes even creepier?

"Um, what?" you ask?

Let me explain.

On a beautiful October afternoon, my wife and I dressed our daughter up in a very cute costume and hopped in the car to go to a local church's "trunk-or-treat." If you are unfamiliar with this kind of event, it is basically a church version of tailgating, sans the alcohol, but with lots and lots of candy corn and inflatable jumping castles. Oh, and clowns.

Clowns and very large stuffed animals freak my little girl out. When I say freak her out, I mean "run like a wild carnivorous gorilla who has not eaten in three weeks chasing you through a mall full of angry lions while senior citizens in their walking class look on" freaking out.

To give you the back story, it all started with Chuck E. Cheese. When our daughter was about a year and a half old, my wife and I took her on the first trip to the land of the giant rat. Everything was great and she was having a blast until the rat made an appearance. I am still convinced that she must think that her parents must have lost their minds taking her to a place where an eight-foot-tall rat lives. In fact, when you think about it that way, she had a pretty good reason to freak out.

And for some reason, clowns seemed to just become a natural manifestation of this fear. I'm not sure why, but even the mention of a clown gets us a very stressed-out toddler on our hands.

So back to our alcohol-free tailgating party that ends in a sugar stupor rather than a football game. It had been several months since we had to encounter anything in costume (we have gotten pretty good at avoiding all eight-foot-tall rats) or any clowns (although we once ran into one in the mall nowhere near October, which was weird in and of itself), so we were hopeful that her almost-comical fear of clowns and very large stuffed animals had passed.

It had not.

As soon as we entered the church grounds, we headed for the jumping castles to try and break the ice. My daughter and her best friend Allie Grace were jumping, and we were watching them through the netting when it happened. A well-meaning, costumed volunteer who had somehow gotten the idea that three-year-old children would really enjoy clowns stepped up to the microphone (another thing that scares my daughter, but that's another story for another book) and started talking. Well, to be honest, he was one of those guys who has missed the point of an amplification system altogether and was screaming into the microphone. I was a little scared myself. But at about that time I saw my daughter's face change. A mood of seriousness came over her and her legs started moving, very fast. Her body was not as convinced of the need to move as her legs, so she basically nose-planted into the bottom of the castle while her legs kept moving. She then saw a glimmer of hope—the hole in the castle that serves as its exit. I have never seen anyone, much less a three-year-old, move this fast. I took off to the hole to catch her, and I caught her in my arms just as she dove out.

I am convinced that she would have clawed her way out of a titanium box to get away from the amplified dude with a big red nose and big red feet. She was serious about escaping this danger. She was willing to do whatever it took because she perceived this threat as real, a dangerous threat to her life.

Do you ever wish that you took sin as seriously as my daughter takes clowns with microphones?

Jesus did.

To be fair, Jesus is speaking specifically about adultery here in this passage, but I believe that the principle of avoiding sin at all costs is general. It also is easy for us to think of that "sin that eats your lunch" in stereotypical ways like sex, drugs, and rock and roll. But I think because all sin sends you to the same hell, Jesus is pretty much an equal opportunity hater of all sin.

What was really going on here was that Jesus noticed that people were not scared, flat-out terrified by sin's possible effects on our lives.

Have you ever found yourself starting to loosen your standards when it comes to a sin in your life? We like to rename sin, call it cute names like "issues," "habits," "slip-ups," "stuff we are dealing with," and so on. You know the drill, and you probably have your own pet names for your sin as well. We are guilty of desensitizing ourselves to a point that we are not only ceasing to make progress on our sin, we truly begin to believe it's not sin at all.

What Jesus desires from each of us is that we take our sin very seriously.

Serious as a Heart Attack

He uses hyperbole again in this passage to illustrate just how seriously. He even goes to the extreme of suggesting that we take off a body part, say a hand or an eye, if it causes us to stumble.

We could take this hyperbole literally I guess, but my question then would be "So, Jesus, what happens when I don't have any limbs left to cut off?" Because I don't know about you, but it seems that I am often finding myself back in the same battles with the same sin, and I only have so many arms and legs. What's even more dangerous is that a lot of my sin—the sins of a lot of people, in fact—happens in the mind. We would be talking about a lobotomy. That is serious stuff.

God likes to show me my sin in unusual ways. Like as I have been writing this chapter, I made the mistake (or perhaps the wise decision) of reading this verse right after snapping at my wife. I have renamed this sin of jerkiness stuff such as "being frustrated after a hard day" or "venting." It is just sin, and it is a sin against the woman that I love the most.

As I was thinking through the implications of this verse I thought to myself, "what if I had to get rid of the body part that causes my sin?"

That would mean that I would have to cut my tongue out of my mouth. That would certainly shut me up. It's harsh, but maybe

Jesus is onto something here. Then God reminded me that the real problem is not my tongue but my heart.

We can lose a tongue and still live, but our hearts we really need. The truth is, most of our sin can be traced back to our hearts.

What Jesus is really suggesting here is a radical heart transplant.

Have you ever gotten really bad news from the doctor? Maybe it was a loved one who got it and you lived through it alongside.

I remember waiting for the inevitable phone call after my grandfather had experienced some heart pains. We knew that something would have to happen. You always want but never really expect the doctor to call and say that the pain in your chest was nothing to worry about. When the phone rang, however, we all knew that it was the doctor. We all knew that his news would probably mean surgery, yet we were all surprised when he actually said the words. It was like a wasabi punch to the throat.

Let me wasabi punch you in the throat. This is Jesus talking in Luke 6:43-44 (NLT):

A good tree can't produce bad fruit, and a bad tree can't produce good fruit. A tree is identified by its fruit. Figs never grow on thorn bushes, nor grapes on bramble bushes.

I don't know you, but I am willing to bet the farm (or at least my three-bedroom abode in a middle-class, suburban planned community) that you have produced some bad fruit. Now we can act like it's just semi-rotten fruit if you want, but the standard is perfect and you fail. The news, like that news we got from the doctor, is bad and basically your heart is evil to the core and you have some major heart issues.

Evil to the core. I have not been around a long time, but in my thirty-five years here are a few things I have learned about the human heart.

We Have Heart Disease

A good person produces good things from the treasury of a good heart, and an evil person produces evil things from the treasury of an evil heart. What you say flows from what is in your heart.

Luke 6:45 (NLT)

Did you catch that last line? What we say (and I would infer "do") comes from our heart. It is there and living in our hearts even before we say it. That action is within us even before we do it. We have heart disease.

When my grandfather was diagnosed with that heart disease he seemed like a healthy man. Still in his early fifties and very active, one day he was rushed from work to the hospital with chest pains. After running some blood tests, the doctors determined that he had experienced a heart attack. He had a diseased heart. But that disease did not just start when they ran the tests—it started way before. I would guess if I had to that it started when he ate eggs, bacon, and grits every single morning and smoked a pack of cigarettes for thirty-five years.

The pain was simply a symptom of an already existing issue.

Your pain and your sin are symptoms of a major heart issue. The fact that you are hurt and that you hurt other people is a symptom of a major heart issue. The fact that there is relational carnage all around you is a symptom of a major heart issue. The fact that you cannot seem to kick a habit or hang-up is a symptom of a major heart issue. The fact that you don't take your sin seriously is a product of the fact that it lives inside of you and is a part of you. It's already there. It is in your heart.

The hard reality is that there are really only two categories of people in the world—God and bad (not good and bad). And I am not sure if you are aware, but you are not God.

See, I know for me, if there are "good" and "bad" categories then I am really quick to start thinking of myself as a shoo-in for the "good" category. But when I know the choice is between God and bad, I am reminded that I am evil. And so are you.

> *For I was born a sinner—yes, from the moment my mother conceived me.*
>
> *Psalm 51:5 (NLT)*

All you have to do is be around a one-year-old to know that this happens pretty quickly. I have two children, and they both come by the whole evil thing with no help at all. I have never sat down with my children and taught them "how to be an evil person 101." They just did it naturally.

I remember one of the first times that I saw evil come out in my little girl, Isabelle. She was playing with her best friend Allie Grace when they were both about eighteen months old or so. Both are very sweet girls. Both are inherently evil. Sweet and evil, boy, do I have some tough times ahead.

So the two princesses were playing in the backyard when I saw my daughter eyeing a toy that her friend had in her hands. Like a cheetah, she crept up very slowly behind her friend, waiting for just the right moment, when all of a sudden she snatched the toy from Allie's hand and took off running at an unbelievable speed. Seriously, I am not sure that I have ever seen a child run that fast. This was planned evil. But then as her friend got up and chased her, I saw the real evil come out as my daughter reared back and started hitting Allie over the head with the toy.

I can confirm that my wife and I have never hit anyone over the head with anything in front of our daughter—it came naturally to her. You know why? Because she is a princess, but she is an evil little princess. So are you. So am I. Well, not the princess part— the evil part, though.

And here is the problem when Jesus starts suggesting amputation and such: the problem is our heart. You can cut your arms off, your legs, your tongue off, and gouge your eyes out until you are just a torso, but you will still have a heart. What Jesus is really suggesting here is that we trace the source of our sin back to the origin and eradicate that from our lives.

That is taking sin seriously.

Yet we still try and act like our heart is good. We think that Jesus does not know us. We think we can hide our heart disease from him. What makes Jesus such a great heart surgeon is that he already knows us. Jesus has access to our heart that only he can see. He can take a photo of our lives and show us where we need to get some disease extracted. When you truly know someone, you have the ability to sympathize and look into that person's heart.

My wife and I took our daughter to a local strawberry festival a couple of years ago with two other families. It is a pretty cool deal. There are lots of rides and plenty of strawberries to eat as well. We got to the end of our time there, and we wanted to ride the Ferris wheel before we left. My wife and daughter were getting on the Ferris wheel along with our neighbors and the other friends, and my job was to take pictures. Not just any pictures, but good pictures. This would be a memory we would want to last for a long time. So the pressure was on. When the first bucket came by, I got real close and down low and took pictures of our friends. A quick check of the digital camera showed me that I was getting good pics, doing my job. Then I took some pictures of our neighbors, getting even closer this time, down on one knee. I was working it. Then I took some pictures of the next bucket, with my wife and daughter in it. By now I was feeling very confident and starting to get in for some very close shots and artistic angles and such. Next I sized up bucket number four. I leaned in really close—almost touching the face of the child—when I realized I had no idea who I was taking pictures of—I did not know them. When we got home and saw the picture, it was classic. The mom was looking at me like "why is this guy taking a picture of my daughter and me? Security!" I did not know her, and I think it kind of freaked her out.

Would you agree that it is tough to get counsel from someone who does not know you? When someone gets in your personal space or tries to speak into the deep dark areas of your life, and snap a picture of your soul, it is weird if that person is a stranger.

But Jesus gets you. He understands you. He can relate to you. He already knew that your heart was evil to the core when he died for you. Yet, even though he knows you (yes, even all the evil parts of you that you think you are hiding from him), he also cares for you enough to give you a new heart.

We Need a Heart Transplant

The concept of heart transplantation dates back to at least A.D. 400 in China. It seems humans have known for quite some time that we need to get rid of bad hearts. But the first heart successfully transplanted into a human occurred in 1964 at the University of Mississippi Medical Center in Jackson, Mississippi. A team led by Dr. James Hardy transplanted a chimpanzee heart into a dying patient. The heart beat for seventy minutes before stopping.

People need a good heart. People want a good heart.

You need a good heart. You want a good heart.

I have truly never met anyone who had absolutely no desire to be good. I am sure they exist, but the chance that a complete psychopath would be reading this book is quite unlikely, so I am going to go with a whim and say that you want to be good. Admittedly, "good" has been defined in a variety of different ways, but in some way we all want to live better than we currently live.

This is why we are inspired by the charity campaigns and want to give back through telethons.

This is why we make New Year's resolutions and try our best to eat less, drink less, cuss less, and live less out of our sinful nature.

Because though we may not want to admit it, in the core of our being, we all know that we are inherently evil. We know that we all fall quite short.

For all have sinned and fall short of the glory of God.
Romans 3:23

For most of our lives, we have been lied to and told that we are inherently good, that we were born morally neutral and learn and build on this blank slate a list of evils. But the truth is, we are all pretty jacked up. Some are more jacked up than others. Some learn more evils than others, but Jesus knew the truth—that if we do not eradicate our evil hearts, we are toast.

You see, this verse would have read a lot differently if Jesus thought we could save our hearts with a little spiritual cardio. Rather than cutting off our arms, he would have told us to do some curls and buff ourselves up to resist temptation. He would have suggested an exercise routine to tune our hearts up. You know, do some good, read some Bible, attend some church, and maybe throw an extra 2 percent or so in the offering plate just for good measure.

But a tune-up for a heart that is rotten is a waste of time. We are just going through the motions. Our problem is so bad that Jesus knew we would need to rip our hearts out of our chests. We need to have our hearts of stone removed as Ezekiel 11:19 tells us and replaced with a heart of flesh. Now that is a wasabi punch to the gut.

How to Rip Your Heart From Your Chest

I have a miniature dachshund named Louise. If you have ever been around miniature dachshunds, they are a pretty yappy breed. I was reading online recently that the dachshund breed was known in its wild days for being pretty ferocious. If it felt threatened by a large animal, it would run under the bigger stronger animal, find the soft shallow part of the animal's chest, and with its pointy snout jump up and literally rip the heart out of a bigger enemy.

That is some messed up stuff.

You too have an enemy. It is your own heart. If you know that your heart is bad, the only choice is to rip the heart out of your chest. I guess you could say it's letting the spiritual dachshund out in all of us—or something like that.

Jesus is asking us to change everything we are and take on a new heart. The word *heart* as we translate it in English was the Hebrew word for the "center of our emotions." I think of it as the very core of our soul. It's that piece of you that is, well, "you."

I once met a man who had been extremely disfigured in a horrible accident. There was very little of his body left that was really his. A culmination of plastics, skin grafts, and artificial limbs had rebuilt his body. He had no brain damage or cognition loss at all, however. He was the same person inside. He was 30 percent of his original body but 100 percent of his original soul. People who knew him prior to the accident would remark that one of the strangest parts of the journey had been hearing him speak and knowing that the voice was the same, the sense of humor was the same, but the body was so very different.

So many times we try and deal with our sin by changing our bodies. We change the way we dress (which is a good thing sometimes). We change the way we drink. We change whom we hang out with. We cut off people from our lives. We cut off access to sin. We cut off anything we can to avoid actually dealing with our soul. Our Christian culture today has made soul-change sound absolutely benign.

Say a prayer.

Ask Jesus to come into your heart (still your bad heart, mind you).

Wear a "God's Gym" T-shirt rather than the local bar's.

Do good stuff.

Benign.

Dealing with our soul is extreme.

Jesus knew what he was saying was extreme. He "went there" on purpose. He hoped we would call it crazy. He wanted us to do some extremely crazy stuff to allow him access to our hearts. So crazy, in fact, that the heart transplant Jesus is offering will cost you everything—your entire life. Jesus in another book actually used the words, "carry your cross." In other words, get acquainted with the instrument of death that is the cross and be prepared to carry your own.

I am not sure what that looks like for you. In fact, it is very possible it could indeed look like the very list above (just, please, without the "God's Gym" T-shirt). But what I do know is it is not benign.

It is extreme. It will change you. You will die to yourself. You will live in Christ and you will never be the same.

TAKE A BITE

Many of you still need to allow Jesus to save you. Allow him access to your heart and in doing so, he will give you a transplant and a new heart. I pray that you would get connected in a local church that can help you take that next step. Others of us have had the heart transplant. What we need is an extreme makeover and for Jesus to continue to change us and condition us to have a heart that beats like his father's. A heart that is filled with the DNA of his father and most of all a heart that is good to the core.

I pray also that you would take some extreme measures in your life to make sure that you are growing and learning in community. And then do something special with your new heart, love God and love people and make your life about others. You have a new heart—use it to do something great.

CONCLUSION

The problem with Jesus' words is their absolute clarity and unmoving and unflinching call to extreme action.

The other problem is that, despite their clarity, they are hard to explain.

As an author, I suppose my job is to tie the book up with a nice little bow and give you a recap of the book in this conclusion.

I cannot do that.

Instead, I pray that as God continues to change your heart and soul God will continue to use words written here in some small measure to facilitate that change. But I am not naive enough to think we have solved our problems in one book.

Part of the problem with Christ-followers in the twenty-first century is our need for speed and closure. Someone has convinced us that we have to get closure on everything (let's just blame it on Oprah) and that we can get to that closure very fast (let's blame that one on Dr. Phil, just to be fair). That is a lie.

The chapters in this book attempt to touch on a few of the more radical sayings of Jesus. In this book I also attempt to paint a picture of words that, when applied to our lives, will radically change us. That has been a struggle.

Many times I felt defeated, because I could not give exact prescriptions of how to live in response to these wasabi scriptures. (Forgive me; I am a "high D" personality and like to solve problems. This frustrates my wife, and it frustrated me during this writing.)

The bottom line is that there are no words that can truly describe what Jesus is asking of us in most of these verses. I don't think that means we should not try; in fact, maybe that is what Paul meant when he challenged us to "work out our salvation." Writing this book was a continuation in that working out for me—I hope reading it was for you as well.

If we will allow Christ to work on us and change us, more can be done with us and through us than we could ever ask or imagine. There is more potential in the few people who will read this book than we could ever believe. You don't have the ability or power to do squat. But he does.

I hope he punches you to the gut and you feel it for a lifetime.